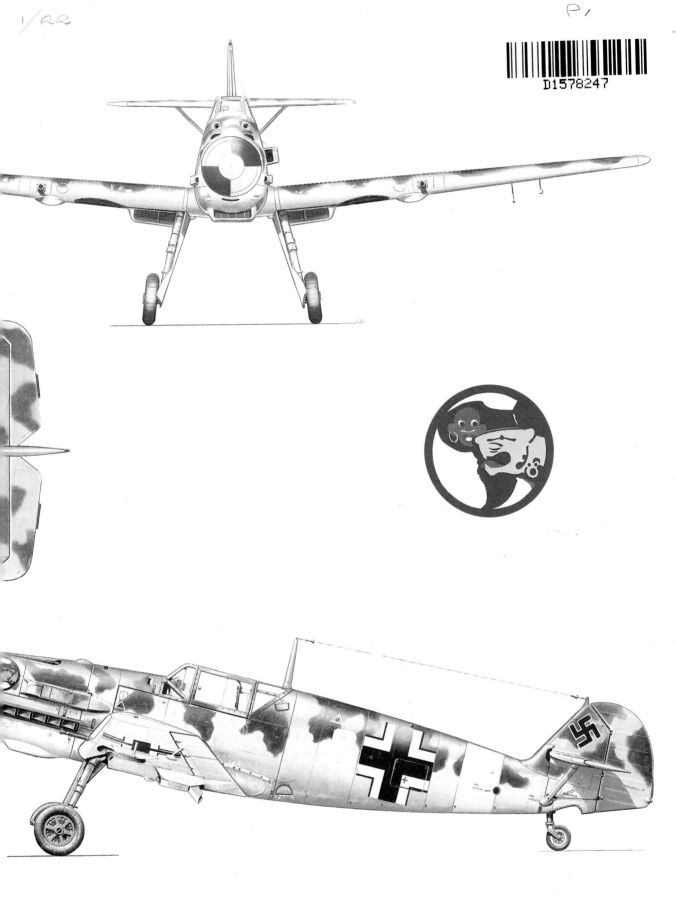

The Fighting Me 109

The Fighting Me 109

Uwe Feist

ARMS AND
ARMOUR

First published in Great Britain in 1988 by Arms &
Armour Press Ltd., Artillery House, Artillery Row,
London SW1P 1RT.

Distributed in the USA by Sterling Publishing Co. Inc.,
2 Park Avenue, New York, NY 10016.

Distributed in Australia by Capricorn Link (Australia) Pty.
Ltd., P.O. Box 665, Lane Cove, New South Wales 2066.

British Library Cataloguing in Publication data

Feist, Uwe, *1937–*
The fighting Me 109,
1. Messerschmitt BF. 109 aeroplanes, 1934–1945
I. Title
632.74'64

ISBN 0-85368-961-X

Edited and designed at Little Oak Studios,
Typeset by Typesetters (Birmingham) Ltd.
Printed and bound in Great Britain by
Richard Clay Ltd, Chichester, Sussex.

Jacket illustration from a painting by Uwe Feist.
Endpaper illustrations reproduced from paintings in the
collection of N. Paul Whittier.

Contents

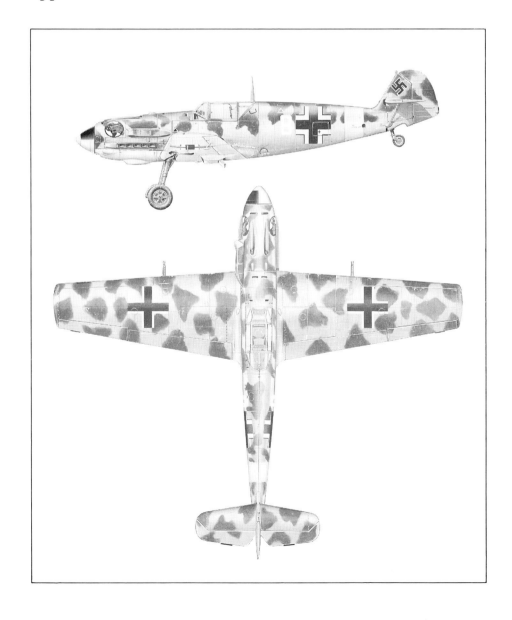

Introduction

Legendary is too strong an adjective to apply to any but a handful of aircraft. The Bf 109 stands out even among this short list, having earned a reputation in the Second World War that makes Messerschmitt a household word to this day. Whatever its relative merits compared to the British Spitfire or the American P-51 Mustang, the Bf 109 has the distinction of having been flown by the highest-scoring fighter aces in history. Rugged, fast and heavily armed, it fought a long and bitter war.

While a great deal has been written about the Bf 109 (also called the Me 109), most sources concentrate on the technical aspects of the aircraft and provide little insight into its wartime use. This volume, presenting as it does a historical survey, attempts to redress the balance. The book also portrays the men who flew Germany's formidable fighter, superb photographs – many of them very rare – complementing a discussion of the hardships and day-to-day life of the front-line *Luftwaffe* pilots. Theirs was a six-year war of attrition without the luxury of a fixed tour of duty: they flew as long as they were able, with no maximum number of missions and little hope of regular leave to return to their homes. Facing prolonged stresses greater than those suffered by any other group of pilots in history, they fulfilled their military duty despite crippling shortages, numerical inferiority on both fronts and the growing inevitability of defeat. Most rejected the Nazi ideology, and all were accused of cowardice by an irrational high command disenchanted with its *Luftwaffe*.

Out of these difficulties there emerged the great aces, with scores so high as to be almost incredible. Hartmann, Barkhorn, Rall, Obleser, Steinhoff, Krupinski, Bär . . . More than one hundred *Luftwaffe* pilots each scored over a hundred aerial victories. Fifteen scored over two hundred, two scored more than three hundred, and top ace Erich Hartmann brought down almost six times as many aircraft as the highest-scoring pilot of any other nation. Heinz Bär was shot down on eighteen occasions, yet climbed back into the cockpit every time.

First flown in 1935, the Bf 109 was obsolescent during the latter half of the Second World War, yet it remained the backbone of the *Luftwaffe*'s day fighter force. Never completely superseded by the excellent Focke-Wulf Fw 190, it was in production up to the end of hostilities and, with some 33,000 examples built, is second only to the Soviet 'Sturmovik' as the most prolific design in the history of military aviation. Perhaps the greatest testimonial to its qualities is the fact that 'old hands' with scores of victories to their credit refused to relinquish it: almost all the top aces preferred their trusty '109s' right to the end.

Photographs appearing in this volume have been supplied by W. Held, A. Parker, R. Hirsch, E. Maloney, K. Rieger, U. Bischof, B. Meyer and J. Koral, and by the NASM, H. Roosenboom and Uwe Feist Archives.

Uwe Feist

◀ **A Bf 109F-2 of** *III Gruppe/JG 53* **flown by** *Lt.* **Erich Schmidt, 1941.**

Development and History

The design of the Bf 109 fighter began under rather inauspicious circumstances, surrounded by personal conflicts between Willy Messerschmitt, co-manager of the Bayerische Flugzeugwerke AG (BFW), and the State Secretary of Aviation, Erhard Milch. Their animosity had resulted from an earlier episode, when BFW had been forced into bankruptcy in 1931 by the cancellation of a contract issued by Deutsche Lufthansa, of which Milch was then Managing Director. Although BFW had been resurrected in 1933, with Messerschmitt as a co-manager, and Milch had been appointed to his new position, the relationship between the two had not improved. Milch could not prevent production contracts from being issued to BFW, although he did manage to disparage Messerschmitt's efforts and attempted to restrict BFW's production to the manufacturing of other companies' designs. Accordingly, with no official development contracts forthcoming, Messerschmitt attempted to hold his design group together by seeking work from foreign sources, and in mid-1933 a development commission was secured from Romania for a commercial transport; design work was also initiated on a light monoplane, the M-37, in which the Romanian airline had expressed interest. The acceptance of this development contract from a foreign source soon brought an official reprimand from the Technical Office (*C-Amt*) of the Air Ministry and additional pressure from Milch. Faced with the facts of the situation, however, the *C-Amt* had to concede the point and awarded a development contract to BFW.

At this time the German aviation industry was attempting to recover from the effects of the First World War and the restrictions which had been imposed upon it by the Treaty of Versailles. Under the treaty, Germany had been forbidden to build aircraft of any type, although this restriction was later relaxed so that civilian aircraft could be produced. Interest in the field of aviation had grown rapidly after the end of the war and fostered international flying competitions which greatly influenced potential purchasers for individual manufacturer's products. No small amount of national pride was also at stake in the competitions. A contest was to be held in 1934, and the German government felt this to be an excellent opportunity to display its rejuvenated air industry. Development contracts for machines to represent Germany in this next event were issued to various aircraft companies, and just such a contract was awarded to BFW by the *C-Amt*.

The provisions of the contract called for six examples of a single design to be ready for the contest in August–September 1934, but with less than a year remaining until that date, Messerschmitt was faced with a limited development period for his design, now officially designated Bf 108. Happily, however, the specifications for the competition aircraft were broad enough to allow Messerschmitt's M-37 design to meet the requirements. Since design work had already begun on this project, much precious time was saved and it was possible to begin construction in October 1933, and by the spring of 1934 the first of the six Bf 108As stood ready to begin test flights.

Even though the Bf 108 did not take any of the first places in the 1934 contest, coming fifth, sixth and tenth, its overall performance was impressive. Within the basic aerodynamic design, Messerschmitt had incorporated the very latest techniques – a combination of features which were to remain unique for its class for

◄◄ Professor Willy Emil Messerschmitt was born in Frankfurt-am-Main on 26 June 1898. His father Ferdinand was a wine merchant.

◄ *Generalluftzeugmeister* Ernst Udet during an inspection of the Bayerische Flugzeug-werke, Augsburg, 1937.

◄ A French delegation headed by *Général* Vuillemin, Commander-in-Chief of *L'Armée de l'Air* (French Air Force) during a visit to the Messerschmitt, Augsburg factory as guests of *Feldmarschall* Erich Milch and *General* Udet, August 1937.

◄ Messerschmitt Bf 108 D-IMTT flies over the Bavarian Alps in 1937. Called *Taifun* (Typhoon), this four-seat, low-wing monoplane of 1934 shared many advanced features with the Bf 109 single-seat fighter of 1935, which it closely resembled.

▲ The Heinkel He 112
V9, a close competitor of
the Messerschmitt
fighter.

some time. Most of these same design features were to be found in Messerschmitt's next design and development contract for the Air Ministry, which had been received even before the Bf 108 had made its maiden flight. Specifications issued by the Air Ministry called for the design of a fighter of monoplane configuration, armed with two machine guns synchronized to fire through the airscrew (a third gun might be mounted through the engine), capable of a speed in excess of 280mph (based on projected performance data for the Jumo 210 engine, itself currently undergoing development), and with the emphasis placed on spin behaviour. The specifications released along with the contracts for prototype development had been sent to the larger German aircraft companies such as Heinkel, Fieseler, Arado and Focke-Wulf and to several of the smaller companies, amongst them BFW. Messerschmitt, however, had been informed unofficially that no production contract would be awarded for a BFW fighter if such an aircraft should be produced. Messerschmitt's lack of experience in the design of high-speed combat aircraft seemed to preclude his offering a serious threat to the other, more experienced companies, and if Milch had thought that a threat existed he doubtless would have seen to it that the contract was not sent to BFW.

Against the background of these seemingly insurmountable problems, Messerschmitt and his design staff set out to create the very best aircraft their combined skills could produce. Current convention could be ignored: there seemed to be nothing to lose inasmuch as the future promised no production contract. The team's most recent design experience had centred around the Bf 108, it was only logical that this experience would be carried over into the Bf 109 project. Messerschmitt had, as already noted, combined in the 108 the latest technical features, none of which, however, taken individually, was revolutionary. Thus the Bf 109 took shape on the drawing boards of the BFW Augsburg facility in the summer of 1934 with lightweight, metal-alloy framework and flush-riveted stressed skinning; leading-edge slots on the wings, controlled in conjunction with slotted trailing-edge flaps to increase the wing area; a fully retractable main landing gear; a completely enclosed cockpit with a jettisonable canopy; and high-quality cellulose paint to reduce drag. The smaller wing of the 109 brought about a much higher wing loading, 24lb/sq ft, compared to the 20.3lb/sq ft of what would be its closest rival in the design contest, the Heinkel He 112. During the early days of the test and evaluation period this feature was thought to be something of a drawback by the test pilots, but the fears were dissipated during the evaluation tests proper.

The wing layout of the Bf 109 would offer some challenging problems in the future as the need arose to install superior weaponry. At this time the standard armament of fighter aircraft consisted of multiple machine guns of rifle calibre, in approximately the 0.30in range, but during the mid-1930s the armament experts were changing their views about such weapons as evidence had shown that the newer aircraft, of all-metal construction (fabric-covered aircraft were still common), possessed a certain amount of immunity to these guns. A machine gun or cannon of larger calibre seemed to be required, but, curiously enough, when the German Air Ministry released its specifications it called for rifle-calibre MG 17s to be installed; the final weapons layout for the British Spitfire likewise incorporated eight 0.303in machine guns.

Designing his aircraft to the specifications set forth by the Air Ministry, Messerschmitt had made the wing of the 109 thin, with the main spar at about the mid-chord point, which was acceptable since no wing armament was required; by way of comparison, both the Spitfire and Hurricane had provisions for the installation of their armament in the wings from the outset. The location of the 109's wing spar and the lack of thickness to the wing itself would necessitate many ingenious modifications in order to fit heavier firepower within these limitations, and most of the protuberances, blisters and other bulges found on the later models of the Bf 109 resulted from the efforts made to upgrade the original design in order to incorporate an increased armament and larger powerplants.

Preliminary tests

In August 1935 the first Bf 109 was completed and began a series of preliminary trials prior to being taken to the Air Ministry's official test station at Rechlin. Registered D-IABI, the Bf 109 V1 ('V' indicating *Versuchs*, or test) had initially been fitted with a Rolls-Royce Kestrel V12 liquid-cooled engine of 695hp, those engines available within the German aircraft industry being heavyweight types intended for commercial use: under the conditions of the Versailles Treaty, Germany had been forbidden to develop aircraft engines of a 'military' character, and though such powerplants were begun with the Jumo 210 and Daimler-Benz DB 600 (which were to be interchangeable in the fighter), their development remained some time behind that of the fighters themselves. Rolls-Royce had recent experience with high-performance engines of this type, having produced the racing engines for the Supermarine aircraft that participated in the Schneider Trophy contests, and securing import models of the Rolls-Royce Kestrel and substituting them for the Jumo – chronologically the more advanced of the two German designs, so much so that Focke-Wulf had in fact received an example for use in its entry – allowed initial tests involving the various fighter designs to be carried out. No definite decision was to be made until trials could be conducted with the specified powerplant; nevertheless, the Bf 109 V1 proved to be the fastest of the entries, by a margin of some 17mph over its closest competitor, the He 112.

In the meantime, construction work was proceeding on the second and third prototypes, the Bf 109 V2, D-IUDE, and the Bf 109 V3, D-IHNY. In October 1935 the Jumo 210A engine became available and was installed in the V2, but because of delays in the delivery of powerplants the V3 would not be ready until June 1936. The differences between the V2 and V1 models were minor, some strengthening being carried out on the landing gear of the V2 and provision being

► Messerschmitt Bf 109 V3 *Werk Nr.* 760, D-IOQY, was fitted with an engine-mounted MG 17 machine gun.

► Bf 109 C-1s lined up at the Messerschmitt factory in 1938.

109-Serie vor dem Abflug

► A Messerschmitt Bf 109B-1.

made for the installation of the two machine guns in the nose; the V3 model would be the first actually to have these weapons installed.

Flight tests of the Bf 109 V2 and its 610hp Jumo 210A engine began in January 1936. By the time the final competitive trials were held at Travemünde in the autumn of 1936, Arado's Ar 80 and Focke-Wulf's Fw 159 had fallen by the wayside and only Heinkel's He 112 was in the running. Messerschmitt's Bf 109, piloted by *Dr.-Ing.* Hermann Wurster, put on a remarkable demonstration, proving its superiority, and it was selected as the standard German fighter.

Shortly before this time, and the decision to standardize on the Bf 109, the *Reichsluftfahrtministerium*, (RLM, or Air Ministry), had changed its official views concerning the Bf 109 to the extent that a contract was placed with BFW to build ten examples of a pre-production fighter. This series would be known as the Bf 109B-0, and would be used for further test purposes. As such, all in this series were allotted 'V' numbers, the first B-0 being the Bf 109 V4, the second the Bf 109 V5, and so forth.

Apart from the outstanding performance shown by the Bf 109 during the test evaluation period, in the light of which the final decision had been made, outside factors were at work. Supermarine's fighter, the Spitfire, had flown for the first time on 5 March 1936. The British Air Ministry was favourably impressed, and it awarded a production contract for 310 machines in June of that year. The rapidity with which Britain adopted the Spitfire and the close similarities in performance between it and the Bf 109 provided additional food for thought for the RLM. Moreover, in June 1936 the Air Ministry had also placed a contract order for six hundred Hawker Hurricanes. The armament for this new aircraft, eight machine guns, was identical to that of the Spitfire but heavier than that which the RLM had specified for its fighter design. Possibly because of this revelation, the RLM quickly

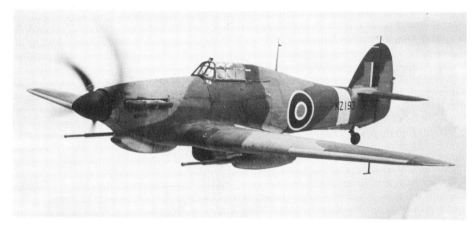

◄ A Hurricane Mk. V with a heavy underwing cannon armament. The RAF preferred to use the Hurricane – an excellent gun platform – for attacks on bombers or ground targets rather than against the Bf 109, to which it proved markedly inferior.

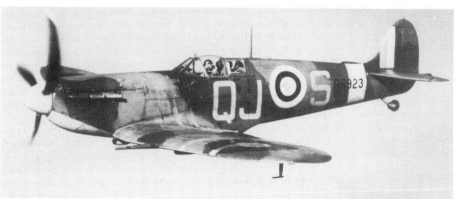

◄ This Supermarine Spitfire flew with No. 92 Squadron at Manston. Built as Mk. I but upgraded to a Mk. Vb, it entered service just after the Battle of Britain.

► The Bf 109B-2 was powered by a Jumo 210Da engine with fuel injection.

revised its requirements and called for the installation of a third MG 17 to fire through the airscrew shaft of the Bf 109. All three MG 17s were supplied with 500 rounds of ammunition, of 7.92mm calibre. The request for this modification came shortly before the close of the official trials at Travemünde, the Bf 109 V4 flying with the full three-machine-gun installation in November 1936. The following month the V5 and V6 models appeared. These differed from the V4 in that a Jumo 210B engine was installed and minor revisions were made to the wheel wells, canopy and machine-gun air intakes. The improved Jumo 210B retained the same power rating as the 210A for take-off but afforded greater power at high altitude and raised the service ceiling of these models.

Combat conditions

One of the next steps in the development of the 109 took place in Spain. In July 1936 General Franco had sent representatives to Germany to discuss the possibility of securing German aid for his forces in the Spanish Civil War, the Nationalists. Hitler's response was to form the Condor Legion, through which he expressed his support for Franco's cause and served notice that he intended that the Nationalists should triumph, at the same time not only providing him with an opportunity to fight his acknowledged foes, the Bolsheviks, but also giving the new *Luftwaffe* (which had been officially created on 1 October 1934) a chance to try out its tactics and new equipment under combat conditions. The first volunteers, together with

► The first shipment of Bf 109Es arrived in Spain in early 1939.

15

◄ Heinkel He 51A-0s fly in formation in the spring of 1934. These biplane fighters, shown here with civil registrations for the manufacturer's tests, would be the first German aircraft to participate in the Spanish Civil War two years later.

◄ The Polikarpov I-15 first flew in 1933. The Soviet biplane fighter participated in the Spanish Civil War, where it proved to be easy prey for the greatly superior Messerschmitt Bf 109.

◄ An abandoned I-16 with an ammunition belt dangling from the fuselage.

six Heinkel He 51 biplane fighters, had in fact already been despatched in July, but with the official formation of the Legion in November open recruitment was conducted from within the ranks of the *Luftwaffe*. Several future German aces cut their combat teeth during this struggle, among the more notable being Mölders, Galland and Trautloft.

The initial successes with the He 51 soon slackened as Soviet-supplied Polikarpov I-15 fighters arrived in increasing numbers in support of the Republican side, and it was with a view to reversing this change in fortunes that the Bf 109 V4 was sent to Spain in December 1936, joined the following month by the V5 and V6. Two months of combat flying – not of a continuous nature, for these were experimental models – clearly demonstrated the performance characteristics of the 109 to be superior to those of the aircraft being flown by the Republican forces, after which the trio of Messerschmitts were returned to Germany to continue their participation in the overall development programme of the 109.

The first full-production military version of the 109, the Bf 109B-1, began leaving the assembly lines in February 1937. Two *Gruppen* (Groups) of the *Luftwaffe*'s *JG 132*, *Jagdgeschwader 'Richthofen'* (Fighter Wing 'Richthofen'), were earmarked to be the first to convert to the new aircraft, and after a hasty conversion course personnel from *II/JG 132* were sent, along with the 109B-1, to join the 2nd *Staffel* (squadron) of *Jagdgruppe 88* (Fighter Group 88), one of the units of the Condor Legion. These B-1s arrived in Spain in April 1937 and were followed in August by some of the first of the new B-2 models, supplied to re-equip the 1st *Staffel* of *J/88*. New features in the B-1 model included the 680hp Jumo 210Da engine, a Reflexvisier (Revi) IIIa reflector gun sight, and short-range, 30–35-mile radio equipment, the FuG 7 (*Funkgerät*, or radio set) transmitter/receiver. Approximately thirty B-1s were produced before the B-2 model entered the assembly line. An initial difference between these two models was the replacement of the wooden, fixed-pitch Schwarz airscrew with a metal, two-bladed, variable-pitch propeller, a VDM licence-built version of the American Hamilton Standard. B-1s were retrofitted with the VDM airscrew. The two Bf 109B-equipped *Staffeln* of *J/88* amassed an impressive record. The 3rd *Staffel* obtained Bf 109Cs and Ds in April 1938; the 4th *Staffel* was formed in mid-1938 but kept the He 51 for close assault work.

Despite the limited numbers of Me 109s in service, it did not take long to verify what had already been hinted at with the Bf 109 V4, V5 and V6: the Republican-flown, Soviet-built I-15s and I-16s were no match for the German aircraft. The combat reports returning from Spain were important to Messerschmitt's designers and engineers. Shortcomings which appeared could be taken into consideration and improvements made within a shorter time span than would have been possible had the aircraft stayed at home, and as newer models were produced, batches of these would be forwarded to the Condor Legion for practical operational evaluation. A total of 136 Bf 109s were sent to Spain during the conflict, but April 1939 saw the Germans begin to return home. Behind them they left much of their equipment, including twenty-seven surviving Bf 109B and C models along with twenty of the very latest E model. The pilots returned with priceless combat experience – experience which would soon be put to use once more.

After the return of the Bf 109 V4 in March 1937, armament tests were begun in an effort to remedy inadequacies found in the B model. A combination of problems associated with cooling and vibration meant that the trial installation of a 20mm MG FF/M firing through the airscrew could not be viewed as a success, and additional work would be necessary before it could be relied upon. The question of a powerplant was not entirely resolved either. As a prototype of the B-2 series, the Bf 109 V7 had been fitted with the VDM airscrew and the powerplant, a Jumo

210G of 700hp, featured direct fuel injection in an attempt to overcome difficulties with the carburettor. Delays in the production of the Jumo 210G saw the B series completed with the 210Da engine, the G version seeing service with the next model of the 109, the C.

Demonstrating the potential

The Fourth International Flying Meeting, held in Zurich in July–August 1937, afforded the Germans a chance to demonstrate their abilities in the aeronautical field and also the potential of the Bf 109: prior to this, on 16 March 1935, the disarmament clauses of the Treaty of Versailles had been renounced and Germany could once more publicly parade her military might. According to Dr. Goebbels' Propaganda Ministry, the five Bf 109s entered with the German team were standard production aircraft, seeing wide distribution within the new *Luftwaffe*, but while most of the other claims made by the Propaganda Ministry would be borne out by the time the meeting ended, the competition aircraft were not production versions, and at this time the total number of *Luftwaffe* fighter *Gruppen* equipped with the Bf 109 stood at three, none of which were up to full strength. The Messerschmitt line-up comprised the Bf 109 V8 and V9, each fitted with the Jumo 210Ga fuel-injection engine; the V10 and V13, each powered by an early example of the Daimler-Benz DB 600A of 960hp; and a Bf 109B-2 stripped of all armament.

In terms of their performance, the Bf 109s swept the field. *Major* Seidemann, in the V8, won the Circuit of the Alps, completing the 228-mile course at an average speed of 241mph; *Generalmajor* Ernst Udet had also attempted this course in the

▲◄After receiving the superior Bf 109E, pilots of the Condor Legion enjoyed total superiority over the Red Spanish Air Force.
▲►Generaloberst Ernst Udet – First World War ace, dare-devil flyer of the 1930s, inspector of fighter pilots and test pilots, and in charge of aircraft production until his death by suicide on 17 November 1941.

► A Bf 109B-1 soars
against a dramatic
background of clouds
during acceptance trials
in mid-1937.

V10 but had been forced to crash-land after engine failure. A 254mph speed record, flying four times around a 21.4-mile course, was set by Carl Francke, also in the V8, and the same pilot attained top honours in the Climb and Dive Competition with the Bf 109 V13. Finally, flying as a team over the Circuit of the Alps course, the 109s took the first three places, their average speeds being 233.5mph.

Early in their careers, the Bf 109 V8 and V9 had been fitted with the Jumo 210Da engine, while the V10 was flown with the Jumo 210G; all three aircraft were intended as prototypes for the Bf 109C series. Prior to their entry in the flying meet in July–August 1937, all were re-engined and, externally, a redesigned, deeper radiator bath appeared beneath the Jumo 210Ga along with revised exhaust ports. Problems with the engine-mounted MG 17 had not yet been solved, and in an effort to increase the aircraft's firepower weapons testing was carried out on the V8 with a pair of MG 17s mounted in the wings. The results of the tests showed that a certain amount of wing strengthening would be necessary, and after this change

▼ Messerschmitts similar
to this Bf 109B took four
first prizes at the 1937
International Air Meet at
Dübendorf airfield,
Zürich, Switzerland.

had been implemented the four-gun arrangement – two in the fuselage with 500 rounds each and two in the wings with 420 rounds each – became standard in the Bf 109C-1 production model. Additional weapons tests were conducted using the V9, with two 20mm MG FFs mounted in place of the 7.92mm machine guns installed in the V8, but the final results of these trials would not be seen until the advent of the Bf 109E model. Considerable redesign had to be undertaken before the wing-mounted cannon could be incorporated into the airframe and some degree of serviceability achieved, but production of the Bf 109C began in November 1937. The C-3 version appears to have been a standard C model returned to the factory and modified with a new wing mounting the 20mm MG FF. Only about fifty C-series aircraft were built in total.

World records

As the latest mark of Bf 109 began to emerge from the assembly lines in November 1937, new laurels were about to be placed on Willy Messerschmitt's design. On 11 November the Bf 109 V13 increased the world's landplane air speed record to 379.38mph. Flown by *Dr.-Ing.* Hermann Wurster, the V13 had been fitted with a special racing version of the DB 601 engine, which could be boosted to 1,650hp for short periods of time. However, Messerschmitt was not the only German aircraft designer interested in an assault on the world's absolute speed record. Heinkel's failure to have his design, the He 112, accepted by the RLM during the original fighter competitions had prompted his engineering staff to begin work on a new aircraft, intended to be the successor to the Bf 109. This project resulted in the He 100 series. It is interesting to note that the design included a provision for two sets of wings, one for the standard fighter model and a second set, smaller in size, to be used for an attempt on the speed record. On 6 June 1938 the He 100 V3, flown by

◄ *Dr.* Hermann Wurster with his honoured American guest Col. Charles Lindbergh in the cockpit of the Messerschmitt Bf 108 during a visit to Germany in October 1938.

▲ Two of the dozen He 100D-1s built by Heinkel are shown here in flight. Crewed by company test pilots, these pre-production fighters saw aerial combat in an *Industrieschutzstaffel* (industry defence squadron), protecting Heinkel's Rostock-Marienehe factory from Allied bombing.

Generalmajor Udet himself, covered the 100km (62.14-mile) closed-circuit speed course and established a new record of 394.4mph. For reasons of propaganda, the aircraft was not identified as the He 100 but rather as the 'He 112U', to promote the idea that the aircraft was in service with the *Luftwaffe*. Another attempt on the record made on 30 March 1939 by the He 100 V8, this time setting a world's absolute speed record of 463.92mph, and again the aircraft was identified as the 'He 112U'.

Messerschmitt meanwhile had also been working on the design of an aircraft to establish such a record, but neither he nor Heinkel was aware of the other's efforts in this direction. As head of the *Technischen Amtes*, Udet knew of their ambitions but could not disclose this information to either for fear of displaying favouritism. While Heinkel's aircraft had been a prototype for a future fighter series, Messerschmitt's was specifically designed for the record attempt, although when awarding a design and development contract the RLM had specified that this programme should be directly related to improving fighter aircraft for the future. Work on the Bf 209, the official designation of the new Messerschmitt aircraft, had progressed to the point where it was felt that a record attempt could be undertaken in July 1939, and so one can imagine the surprise felt by Messerschmitt when the He 100 V8, flown by Hans Dieterle, succeeded in taking the record in March. Not to be outdone, Messerschmitt immediately had the Bf 209 V1 re-engined with a specially boosted DB 601ARJ, producing 1,550hp but capable of being raised to 2,300hp for a one-minute burst of power. With *Flugkapitän* Wendel at the controls, the Bf 209 V1 flew for the record on 26 April 1939, and raised the figure to 469.22mph.

Once again the Propaganda Ministry clouded the facts by attributing the new record to the 'Bf 109R', in order to suggest that this was a variant of the standard fighter version of the 109. Heinkel, enraged that he had not been informed by Udet of Messerschmitt's plans, prepared to assail the record once again using the He 100 V8. Before such an attempt could be undertaken, however, official orders reached him from the RLM to halt these preparations: having created the impression that the 109 fighter had achieved the world record, the RLM would be placed in an embarrassing position should another fighter prove to be faster. It seems likely, however, that had it not been for the action of the RLM in stopping Heinkel, the record set by the Bf 209 could well have been broken not, as it turned out, thirty years later, but just a few months later in 1939.

► **A 1939, still peaceful setting of Bf 109Cs of *Jagdgeschwader 137*.**

Engine development

It will be recalled that the fighter specifications originally released by the RLM had called for the interchangeable use of either the Jumo 210 or the Daimler-Benz 600 powerplant, although the Daimler-Benz engine was intended to be the one that would eventually power the production fighter. Samples of the DB 600 had been installed in several 109 models, but the newer DB 601 promised even greater results, special racing versions of this engine having won for Germany the world air speed record.

Pre-production models of the Bf 109D series had been ordered in the autumn of 1937. The Bf 109 V14 and V15, of this group, were to serve as development aircraft for the next series, the E, powered by the DB 601. There seems to be some confusion surrounding the armament and powerplant installation of the Bf 109D series. It has been stated that production D models were powered by the DB 600Aa, and that 20mm cannon comprised a portion of the aircraft's armament. However, the latest research on this matter, based on a careful examination of company records and other sources, indicates that the production Bf 109D-1 model was in fact equipped with the standard Jumo 210D engine and armed with four MG 17s, two in the fuselage and two in the wings. A total of 650 examples of the D model were produced, ten being sold to Switzerland and three going to Hungary.

The extra heat created by the more powerful DB 601 engine required a redesign

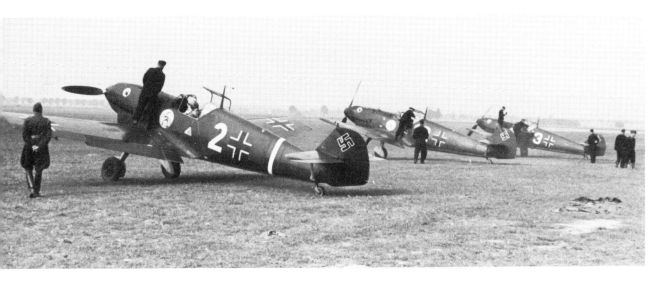

of the production Bf 109, which first came to fruition with the E series. Increasing the cooling area of the radiator would bring about an increase in drag and thus a reduced performance, and so to offset this difficulty two radiators were buried within the wings, only a small oil cooler remaining beneath the engine. Further armament changes were also being considered: the V14 was fitted with two fuselage-mounted MG 17s and two 20mm MG FF cannon mounted in the wings, while the V15 carried only two MG 17s in the fuselage.

By the end of 1938, the production problems afflicting the DB 601 had been overcome and it was released for service use, resulting in the first definitive E series aircraft. The Bf 109E-1, rolling off the assembly lines in early 1939, reached the squadrons in February. Some of the E-1s retained an armament package of four MG 17s, while the rest featured two MG 17s and two MG FF cannon, with 60 rounds per gun, in the wings; other equipment included a three-bladed, controllable-pitch VDM airscrew, a Revi reflector gun sight and FuG 7.

◄ **The Messerschmitt Bf 109 V14 was the second pre-production E-series prototype.**

► **A Bf 109E-1 of** *II/JG 54,* **spring 1939. Replacing the E-1 by late 1939, the Bf 109E-4 had provision for a 20mm MG FF/M cannon firing through the airscrew.**

With the clouds of war gathering on the horizon, production of the Bf 109 was increased from some 400 in the year 1938 to almost 1,100 for the period January–September 1939; of this latter number, more than 300 machines were exported, to Switzerland, Yugoslavia, Romania and a number of other European countries, between April 1939 and April 1940. On the eve of the opening of hostilities, the *Luftwaffe* could count 946 serviceable Bf 109s among its total fighter strength, but even though production had been greatly boosted, neither Messerschmitt's own factories nor those of other manufacturers building Bf 109s under licence were operating at full capacity, nor would they do so for several years: the German leadership apparently did not entirely appreciate what the reaction would be to its proposed operations against Poland, nor did it grasp the magnitude of the role that the Bf 109 would be called upon to play.

▶ Vickers Wellington bombers.

The 'Phoney War'

The Polish campaign was a brief interlude. One of the first objectives had been to knock the Polish Air Force from the skies and, for the most part, this was achieved by *Luftwaffe* bombers attacking the Polish airfields, catching and destroying the greater portion of the aircraft on the ground. Undaunted, Polish flyers took to the air in their remaining obsolescent PZL P.7 and P.11c fighters to challenge German air might, scoring several victories against the 109: over the entire campaign, 67 Bf 109s were listed as losses, although the majority of these fell victim to ground fire.

The first meeting between the RAF and the *Luftwaffe*'s Bf 109 occurred on 4 September 1939, near Brunsbüttel, when a Wellington bomber was shot down while making an attack on the German battlecruisers *Scharnhorst* and *Gneisenau*. The following December saw a force of twenty-four Wellingtons met by a mixed assortment of Bf 109s and Bf 110s. The ensuing battle saw fifty per cent of the attacking RAF force shot down, and three additional Wellingtons crash-landed upon their return to England. This victory for the *Luftwaffe* brought about many changes in the thinking of RAF Bomber Command and the subsequent operations which they were to carry out over Germany. No notable engagements were conducted over the Western Front during the first few months of the war owing to restrictive weather conditions, but the few encounters that did take place between German and British or French aircraft still led the *Luftwaffe* to believe that they possessed the best single-seat fighter in the world.

▶ Maintenance work on the Daimler-Benz DB 601A engine of a Bf 109E-4 of 7/*JG 26* during the Battle of Britain.

Development of the 109 pressed forward, the Bf 109 V17 flying in the summer of 1939 as the prototype for the E-3 series. Efforts were still under way to place a 20mm cannon within the engine, and provision for this had been made in the DB 601Aa; however, no complete solutions had yet been found to the problems caused by vibration and overheating, and although the E-3 had been intended to supplement the E-1 and feature this increased firepower, few of these newer models were seen in service with the engine-mounted 20mm. Production of the Bf 109E-3 began in late 1939, and its DB 601Aa twelve-cylinder, liquid-cooled, inverted-vee engine, rated 1,175hp for take-off, did increase the aircraft's overall performance compared to that of the E-1 model.

The end of the 'Phoney War' came on 10 May 1940 as Germany launched an assault against the Low Countries and France. More than a thousand Bf 109s were made available for use in this theatre, representing almost the complete serviceable strength of the type. In view of the total numbers of aircraft committed to the venture, combat losses were not high, some 235 Bf 109s being destroyed during the May–June battles. The number of combat-available aircraft did decline, however, as problems with logistics increased, and, partly because of this, RAF fighters were able seriously to impede the efforts of Göring's bomber force to wipe out the remaining elements of the British Expeditionary Force on the beaches at Dunkirk.

◄ The canopy of a Bf 109E-1 with added seat armour and an armoured windscreen attachment.

◄ A Messerschmitt Bf 109E-1/B of *JG 26 'Schlageter'*, armed with four 50kg (110lb) bombs.

◄ A 109E of *II Gruppe/ JG 54 'Grünherz'* crash-landed in a French beet field after limping for home with a direct flak hit in the lower fuselage.

The signing of the Armistice with France ended the campaign in the West. Preparations were begun for an attack on Britain, but the attack could not be carried out until losses had been made good and overall strength built up. In the meantime, the results of lessons learned in the fighting began to appear in later production models of the E series. New protection for the pilot – seat armour, and an armoured plate behind his head, attached to a revised canopy – was added to the E-3 models. The engine-mounted 20mm gun was finally abandoned in favour of two wing-mounted MG FFs, and these appeared as standard equipment on the Bf 109E-4, which replaced the E-3 during the latter half of 1940. Difficulties brought about by the limited range of the 109 – another shortcoming of the basic design – had been encountered even in the battles fought by the Condor Legion in Spain, and while this problem would never be completely eliminated, efforts were made to extend the range by adding a 300-litre (79.62 US gallon) fuel tank beneath the fighter.

The possible use of the Bf 109 as a fighter-bomber, or *Jagdbomber* (commonly referred to as '*Jabo*'), had also been considered during the French campaign. Tests were carried out toward this goal, and a number of E-1 machines were modified to carry a single SC 50 bomb* and redesignated Bf 109E-1/B. Some E-4 models were completed straight off the assembly lines to serve in the *Jabo* role and were identified as Bf 109E-4/B, on which the fuselage rack could accommodate either four SC 50 bombs or a single SC 250 bomb. The accumulated results of fighter-bomber missions so impressed the *Luftwaffe* high command that a separate *Jabo Staffel* was ordered to be formed within each *Jagdgeschwader*. A reconnaissance version of the E-4, known as the Bf 109E-5, had the wing-mounted cannon removed and an Rb 21/18 camera installed behind the cockpit. Finally, the installation of the new high-compression DB 601N engine – producing 1,200hp for take-off and capable of being boosted to 1,270hp under emergency conditions – in place of the standard DB 601Aa in the E-4 model saw the birth of the Bf 109E-4/N, while a similarly powered version of the E-5 produced the Bf 109E-6 reconnaissance aircraft.

*Sprengbombe Cylindrisch – a thin-walled, general-purpose, high-explosive bomb, of 50kg weight.

▶ **A Bf 109E-4/B with a single 250kg (550lb) bomb, employed in the anti-shipping role.**

Day of the Eagle

The Battle of Britain opened on 13 August 1940, which had been declared as *'Adlertag'*, the Day of the Eagle, by Göring. Plans for Operation 'Sea Lion', the invasion of Britain, called for German air supremacy, and this was dutifully promised by the *Reichsmarschall*. To ensure such supremacy, however, RAF Fighter Command would have to be destroyed or rendered helpless, but the *Luftwaffe* high command failed to appreciate the British aircraft industry's abiltity to make good the RAF's losses, failed to destroy the early-warning radar stations on the coast, and later, upon directions from Hitler, switched from attacking RAF installations to bombing populated areas as its prime targets. Additionally, the Bf 109 had originally been assigned the role of engaging British fighters in open combat, but

28

after the Bf 110 long-range fighter had proved incapable of defending itself or its bomber charges, 109s were required to protect both the bombers and Bf 110s; furthermore, the limited range of the 109 and the resulting short period of time which could be spent over enemy territory – about twenty minutes – were other handicaps.

The battle wore on as one of attrition, lasting two and a half months. German losses numbered more than 1,700 aircraft, 610 of these Bf 109s; British losses totalled some 1,100. Both sides were battered, and while neither suffered a total defeat, plans for a German invasion had to be put off – and a large number of experienced German fighter pilots had been lost. While limited air attacks would be maintained on the British Isles, the majority of the fighter units began to be withdrawn from the area towards the end of October.

Combat evaluation of the performance of the Bf 109 during the Battle of Britain provided new insights, on the basis of which changes were made in the next model, the F. No immediate requirement existed for a quick transition from the E to the F model, however, and more than a year passed before the first Fs began to appear on assembly lines. During this interim period several additional variants of the E model would be seen. The first of these variants, the Bf 109E-7, entered service in late August 1940, provision having been made to increase its range by the use of a 300-litre drop tank as a standard feature. The earlier use of a drop tank of the same capacity had not worked as well as expected, the tanks having been manufactured from moulded plywood and been subject to leaking after exposure to the elements. A single SC 250 bomb could be carried in place of the drop tank for fighter-bomber duties, and the Bf 109E-7/U2 had armour applied to the most vulnerable areas beneath the aircraft to afford some measure of protection when it was used in the close-support role. The first standard use of the GM 1 nitrous oxide power-boosting system in a 109 produced the E-7/Z model.

As the scope of the war increased, German forces found themselves engaged in many areas and faced with many climates. To meet the needs of aircraft serving in tropical areas, where dusty, sandy conditions could ruin an engine, filters were installed over the supercharger intake. These tropicalized versions of the basic models were identified as the Bf 109E-4/Trop, E-5/Trop, and E-7/Trop. The E-8

▼►A Messerschmitt Bf 109E-7 of 7/*JG 26* with a 300-litre drop tank fitted under the fuselage. *JG 26* operated from Gela, Sicily, flying long-range missions against Malta in April 1940.

◄ A Bf 109E-4/N Trop files over North Africa in the spring of 1941; other aircraft of the *Gruppe* are visible in the background. Forward of the supercharger's sand filter is the insignia of *I/JG 27*.

and E-9 models, which were essentially similar to the Bf 109E-7, appeared in late 1940 fitted with the improved DB 610E engine, offering 1,350hp for take-off. The E-9 photo-reconnaissance aircraft had the wing guns removed and an Rb 50/30 camera installed.

Naval versions

Having been assured by Hitler that no war with Britain would be undertaken before 1944, *Admiral* Erich Raeder, Commander-in-Chief of the German Navy, had laid his plans for the development of the German fleet. Under the provisions of Plan 'Z', the *Kriegsmarine* would be expanded to include four aircraft carriers among the vessels felt to be necessary to challenge the Royal Navy on the high seas. The construction of two of these carriers, *Graf Zeppelin* and *Peter Strasser*, had been started in 1938, but neither would, in the event, be completed. Work on *Graf Zeppelin* was halted when the ship was approximately 85 per cent finished, and on *Peter Strasser* at a much less advanced stage.

The aircraft complement for these carriers was to comprise navalized versions of the Ju 87 dive-bomber and the Bf 109 fighter. Catapult points and an arrester hook were attached to the fuselage of a basic E-1 model, the wing span was increased by

◄ A special dust filter was designed for the Bf 109 in order to protect the supercharger air intake from the fine desert sand.

some two feet, and provision was made for the wings to be folded for stowage on board the carriers. The armament consisted of the fuselage-mounted MG 17s, with either two MG 17s or two 20mm MG FFs in the wings. This naval version of the 109 had been designated Bf 109T, 'T' indicating *Träger*, or carrier. After the suspension of construction work on the carriers, the Bf 109Ts were reconverted to landplane configuration by having the special naval gear removed. A ventral rack was installed to accommodate a 300-litre drop tank, four SC 50 bombs or a single SC 250 bomb, and the aircraft was redesignated Bf 109T-2. Powered by a DB 601N engine, the T-2 had an overall performance comparable to that of the E-4/N. A total of seventy 109Ts were built, sixty by Fieseler and ten by Messer-schmitt. Dwindling in numbers as time passed, these aircraft served throughout the war, the last survivors disappearing at the end of 1944.

Design limit

The purpose of the many modifications carried out on the 109 had been to keep the aircraft 'current', an equal if not better match for any opponent, and the ability of the German aircraft industry to meet these changing needs as rapidly as it did is noteworthy. At first glance it might seem that by making a modification here, or increasing the power of an engine there, performance could continue to be improved for an indefinite length of time. In practice however, this cannot be done. For any weapons system – and the Bf 109 should be considered as such – there is a design limit, at which point the maximum results are achieved from the components available within the design structure: any changes or additions beyond this point will have a detrimental effect. In the case of the 109, this design limit was reached with the introduction of the Bf 109F model in the spring of 1941.

Work on four F-series prototypes – the Bf 109 V21, V22, V23 and V24 – commenced in the spring of 1940. Numerous changes were incorporated into the wing, including redesigned radiators, wing flaps and a shortened overall span. Ten pre-production models, Bf 109F-0s, were built for evaluation. The V21 was fitted with a DB 601Aa engine; the other three prototypes had the DB 601E, the powerplant intended for production versions of the F model. Semi-elliptical wing tips, which could be removed, were provided on the V23 to offset the poor flying

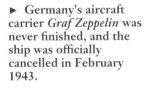

▶ Germany's aircraft carrier *Graf Zeppelin* was never finished, and the ship was officially cancelled in February 1943.

◄ The Daimler-Benz DB 601E engine of a Bf 109F-4/Trop of *JG 27*. This engine produced over 1,300hp, and even more when the GM 1 nitrous oxide pack was installed. The small sign on the cowling is translated as 'Caution when opening. Oil cooler built into cowling'.

▲ A Bf 109F-2 of the *Gruppen* T.O. (group technical officer) of *III Gruppe/JG 3 'Udet'* on the Eastern Front, summer 1941.

characteristics displayed by the V21 and V22. These elliptical wing tips were standardized as part of the wing design in production models of the F and all models of the 109 thereafter. Other changes in the F series included a symmetrical engine cowling, which, in combination with the enlarged airscrew spinner, resembled a bullet; horizontal tail surfaces without the struts of the earlier models of the 109; a new supercharger intake; and a smaller rudder. The fuselage-mounted armament was retained, but provision was made for a 15mm or 20mm MG 151 to be fired through the airscrew shaft.

The first production Bf 109F-1s entered service in November 1940, but the first operational aircraft were grounded after several machines crashed for no apparent reason. Investigation indicated that tail-assembly failure had been the cause of the difficulty, and after appropriate strengthening had been carried out, deliveries were

► With the starter crank in position and armed with four 50kg bombs, this Bf 109F-4/R6 of *JG 54* is ready for action.

resumed. Shortly after the arrival of the F-1, the F-2 model appeared, differing only in having the engine-mounted MG FF/M of the F-1 replaced by the Mauser 15mm MG 151, which was now available in quantity. Production difficulties with the DB 601E had led to the DB 601N engine being installed in the F-1 and F-2 models.

By the time Operation 'Barbarossa', the invasion of the Soviet Union, was under way, almost two-thirds of the fighter units which were to see service in this theatre had converted to the Bf 109F, production of the E model having been phased out by mid-1941. Although overall Bf 109 production had increased from that of the previous year, losses on the Eastern Front made it difficult to keep the total number of fighters available in the *Luftwaffe*'s various areas of operation at an acceptable level, and this drain on 109 fighter strength was not assisted by the fact

that several manufacturers were phasing in production of the new Focke-Wulf Fw 190 fighter, intended to replace the Messerschmitt. Therefore, while the total numbers produced showed a marginal gain, use and demand exceeded supply.

The installation of the GM 1 booster system in the F-2 produced the Bf 109F-2/Z and, as with the E model, the tropical version bore the 'Trop' suffix. These models were followed by the Bf 109F-3, which utilized the DB 601E engine, and the Bf 109F-4, which was fitted with a similar powerplant but had its engine-mounted MG 151 changed from 15mm to 20mm calibre and the ammunition capacity reduced from 200 rounds to 150 rounds.

The fighter-bomber version of the F-4 set out on its first duties during the early weeks of 1942. There was little difference between the Bf 109F-4/B and the standard fighter model apart from the installation of racks for either an SC 250 bomb or four SC 50 bombs. A field conversion kit (*Rüstsatz*) provided a pair of 20mm MG 151 cannon mounted in gondolas under the wings, with 120 rounds of ammunition per gun, to increase the firepower of the fighter when used against bombers, although the flight performance of the aircraft was penalized to some extent with this installation. In such a configuration the fighter became the Bf 109F-4/R1. Other modifications to the F-4 produced the tropicalized version, the

▲ **A Focke-Wulf Fw 190F.**

◄ **A *II Gruppe/JG* 27 Bf 109F-2/Trop with mechanics preparing for a much-needed major engine overhaul, Libya, 1941.**

▲ *Hauptmann* (Captain) Frank Liesendahl's 'Yellow 1', *Werk Nr. 7629.* This Bf 109F-4B flew successfully in anti-shipping missions over the Channel from France during the summer of 1941.

Bf 109F-4/Trop, and the GM 1-boosted Bf 109F-4/Z. Two reconnaissance aircraft were also derived from the F-4: the Bf 109F-5, with the nose cannon removed, a single camera installed and fittings provided for the 300-litre drop tank; and the Bf 109F-6, which had all the armament removed and could carry several different cameras.

'Gustav'

The promised availability of a new Daimler-Benz powerplant, the DB 605A, with 1,475hp at take-off, prompted work on the Bf 109G series. Although this new engine offered more power, the increased weight of the unit itself and the resultant increase necessary to strengthen the fuselage, engine mounts and landing-gear assembly substantially raised the overall weight of the fighter. As had been evident in the previous models, such a change would affect the overall manoeuvrability and handling of the aircraft, but these penalties were felt to be worthwhile considering the higher speeds which could be achieved.

Construction of the pre-production batch of Bf 109G-0s was started during the summer of 1941, and these were followed by the first production model, the Bf 109G-1, in the spring of 1942. The cowling had been recontoured to accept the

► A Bf 109F-5 tactical reconnaissance aircraft taking off for a photo-gathering mission.

DB 605A (which was not installed on the pre-production model because it was not available at the time) and the oil cooler had been enlarged, while an aspect of the changing nature of the air war is illustrated by the fact that a pressurized cockpit had been provided. The armament was at first identical to that of the Bf 109F-4, and the GM 1 nitrous oxide booster system was adopted as a standard feature. The Bf 109G-2, produced almost simultaneously with the G-1, differed only in having the pressurized cabin and GM 1 booster system deleted. Seeing service before the G-1 variant, the G-2 was joined in operations within a short period of time by two additional sub-types, the G-3 and G-4, which were identical to the G-1 and G-2 respectively except for the fact that the FuG 7a was replaced by the newer FuG 16Z.

Modifications were made to a Bf 109G-2 in an attempt to produce a fighter-bomber of extended range. Two 300-litre drop tanks were fitted under the wings and a bomb shackle to carry a SC 500 bomb was mounted beneath the fuselage. The size of the bomb to be carried created clearance problems during take-offs, and to remedy these an auxiliary tail wheel of extended length was fitted beneath and to the rear of the cockpit. Once the aircraft was airborne, the extra undercarriage member was jettisoned by means of explosive bolts fired by the pilot, the wheel parachuting to the ground; upon completion of its mission, after dropping its bomb, the aircraft made a normal landing on its own main gear and integral tail wheel. Much effort was expended on this modification, the Bf 109G-2/R1, and it is surprising to note that no operational missions were flown with the type.

Combat sorties carried out by the Bf 109F in Africa brought back the old problem of malfunctions with the engine-mounted cannon, caused by overheating. With the G model rapidly replacing the existing Fs, a change in armament was

▼ A Bf 109G-2 of 4/JG 54 *'Grünherz'* taxiing on a rain-drenched field landing strip in Russia, 1944.

► The breech blocks of the larger 13mm MG 131 machine gun were enclosed by fairings, giving the G versions a prominent bump on the forward fuselage, christened by its pilots *Die Beule*.

made on the tropical version of the G-1, and a pair of 13mm MG 131 machine guns were fitted in place of the twin MG 17s, with 300 rounds per gun. The large breech blocks of these weapons did not fit easily under the tailored cowling surrounding the DB 605A and necessitated fairings being placed on the cowl to cover them. The theory behind this exchange of weapons was that, in the event of a failure of the 20mm nose cannon, the MG 17s alone were inadequate to destroy an enemy aircraft but the firepower of the 13mm guns could bring about such results. The prominent fairings covering the MG 131s led to the Bf 109G-1/Trop being nicknamed *'Die Beule'* ('The Bump') by air crews and ground personnel alike.

The Bf 109G-5 offered a choice of two distinct powerplants, the DB 605A with a GM 1 booster and the DB 605AS with increased supercharging. The nitrous oxide GM 1 injection had not performed as well as had been hoped on the G model, and removal of the system, which weighed around 400lb, gave some advantage to the DB 605AS. A modification first found on the Bf 109G-5 was an enlarged wooden tailplane. Although the larger area was an advantage, the new tail also weighed more than the standard metal tailplane and required a counterweight added to the nose to maintain the aircraft's balance. This version was designated Bf 109G-5/U2, and later sub-types in the 109 series also received wooden tail units. The armament on the G-5 was identical to that on the G-1/Trop.

Conversion sets, new tactics

For some time the *Luftwaffe* had been working with various types of field conversion sets to increase, as required, its tactical adaptability. The next model in the G series, the Bf 109G-6, was the first model intended to accept these sets, which came from the production line but were not a factory installation. Other changes involved abandoning the pressurized cabin and enabling the airframe to accept a number of different versions of the DB 605A engine, such as the DB 605Am, DB 605D, and DB 605ASCM. These powerplants could be boosted with either the GM 1 system or the new MW 50 water-methanol injection system (the use of either producing additional power but, conversely, causing wear on the engine itself and greatly shortening the life of the ignition system). The twin 13mm machine guns remained in the cowl, along with the 'bumps'. A new Rheinmetall-Borsig 30mm MK 108 cannon was introduced in place of the 20mm MG 151, although a number of G-6s kept the MG 151 because of the poor availability of the MK 108.

The following list will give some idea of the numerous field conversions (*Rüstsätze*) that could be carried out for tactical purposes on the basic G-6 and later K series (and on some earlier models of the G):

R1 ETC 500 bomb rack (carried SC 250 bomb)
R2 ETC 50 bomb rack (carried 4 × SC 50 bombs)
R3 300-litre auxiliary fuel tank
R4 2 × 300-litre fuel tanks
R5 2 × MK 108 30mm cannon
R6 2 × MG 151/20 cannon (in gondolas)
R7 Direction-finding equipment

Factory conversion sets were also to be found in service with G and K series 109s. The majority of these were new tall tailplane assemblies such as that found on the Bf 109G-5/U2, 'U' indicating '*Umrüst-Bausatz*'.

During the early war years, night-fighter tactics had been somewhat slow to develop in Germany. Day fighters had inflicted heavy losses on the RAF Bomber Command, these losses convincing the Command that attacks could be carried out safely only under cover of darkness. Steadily growing night attacks thus started to deliver heavy blows against German targets with many fewer losses on the part of the attacking bombers, and to meet this increasing pressure *Luftwaffegeneral* Kammhuber established a defensive line arranged in some depth and beginning at the Channel coast. Within this 'Kammhuber Line', searchlight and flak batteries were organized to react as a unit, while overhead night fighters were guided to their targets by ground radar stations. At first these fighters were stationed in their own box-like operational sectors, but a major drawback immediately became apparent in that only a limited number of fighters could be directed on to a bomber stream: the defensive line was overpowered when, for example, the RAF mounted its first thousand-plane raid on Cologne on the night of 30–31 May – and matters were to get worse.

In the summer of 1943 a *Luftwaffe* bomber pilot, *Major* Hajo Herrmann, proposed a new plan for night tactics. Bombers were easily silhouetted over target areas from the fire below and from defending searchlights, and, viewed from above, they could be easily attacked. This new tactic became known as '*Wilde Sau*' ('Wild Boar'), and met with considerable success. Three *Geschwader* – *JG 300*, *JG 301* and *JG 302* – were raised to fly such missions, and these units formed *30 Jagddivision*.

▼ **A Bf 109G-5/R6 of *JG* 77 operating from Comiso, Sicily, summer 1943. Underwing gondolas with two MG 151/20 machine cannon plus a 300-litre drop tank lessened the manoeuvrability of the 'Gustav' but added range and punch to the fighter.**

► The Bf 109G-6/R6 had additional underwing 20mm cannon.

► A *JG 3 'Udet'* Bf 109G-5/R1 rolls from its protective tree cover loaded with a single 250kg bomb.

▼ A Bf 109G-5 of 7/*Jagdgeschwader* 27 on long-range patrol over the Mediterranean, September 1943.

They were equipped with the Fw 190F-5/U2 and Bf 109G-6/U4N, the latter being a G-6 fitted with a new tail assembly and a special transmitter-receiver set in the fuselage. In a further attempt to improve the performance of the G-6 for use in night fighting and the *'Wilde Sau'* role, flame dampers and exhaust shielding (to cut glare), additional radio equipment (FuG 25a and FuG 16zy), and the GuG 350 Naxos-Z radar-receiving set were installed in the Bf 109G-6/N. The Naxos gear was capable of picking up British H2S radar emissions at a range of thirty miles and allowed the German fighter to home in on the RAF pathfinders and main bomber formations. The new G-6/N did not see service with *30 Jagddivision*, for the unit was broken up in March 1944, and those models which had been completed were assigned to day-fighter units as replacement aircraft.

The wooden tailplane conversion sets had been introduced in an effort to restore easy handling to the now weighty 109. It was proposed that two of these sets, the U2 and U4, be included as standard assembly-line work in the factory. The product of this modification, as a factory-issue model, was designated Bf 109G-7, but it did not reach assembly production. In a reconnaissance version of the G-6, the Bf 109G-8, the basic model was powered by either a DB 605AS or a DB 605A-1 engine; a single camera was installed, and the 13mm machine guns were removed, leaving the 20mm or 30mm nose cannon. The use of the GM 1 booster or the MW 50 water-methanol injection system resulted in the G-8/U2 and G-8/U3 sub-types respectively.

The Bf 109G-10 airframe standardized on the DB 605D series engine and began to replace the G-6 model on assembly lines in the first quarter of 1944. The MW 50 in the DB 605DC increased the available horsepower of the 605D to 2,000hp for take-off. This engine, with its larger supercharger and MW 50 injection system, produced the fastest version of the G series, with a top speed of 426mph.

▲◄**An 88mm flak battery and searchlights in action during 1943.**
▲▶*Oberst* **Hajo Herrmann advocated night fighter attacks on RAF bombers. Single-engined German fighters would attack the bombers using the illumination provided by searchlights.**

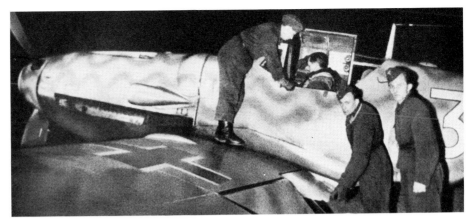

► A Bf 109G night fighter begins a *'Wilde Sau'* operation.

► A home defence Bf 109G runs up at a German airfield. Later in the war, when escort fighters accompanied heavily armed American bombers all the way to the target and back, home defence missions amounted to little more than suicide for the badly outnumbered *Luftwaffe* pilots who flew them.

To attain such speeds, however, it was essential that the aircraft be aerodynamically clean, i.e. unimpaired with outside excrescencies such as the *Rüstsätze*, but, generally, these pieces of added hardware were to be found in service and were accompanied by a decrease in overall performance. The G-10 retained the twin MG 131s but could be fitted with either the 20mm or the 30mm nose cannon. Other differences included new radio equipment, provision for a 300-litre drop tank, and the introduction of the 'Galland hood', a cockpit canopy which improved the pilot's visibility.

The Bf 109G-12 was not a fighter, but rather a training aircraft for future 109 pilots. It had a second cockpit installed behind the original position, the rear portion of the single glazed canopy being bowed out to give the instructor forward visibility on either side of the student pilot's armoured seat directly in front of him. The G-12 was not an assembly-line production model but a conversion from G-1s,

► A Messerschmitt Bf 109G-10/R3 fighter taxiing for take-off.

G-5s and G-6s. The full armament of the original aircraft was generally left in place and a complete set of controls was provided for the instructor. Large numbers of G-12s had been issued to fighter-training-school squadrons such as *JG 101*, *JG 106* and *JG 107* by early 1944, and many were pressed into operational service during the closing stages of the air war over Germany.

The Bf 109K series

The reader may by now have become confused by the maze of Bf 109G-series types and sub-types, and some appreciation, therefore, can perhaps be expressed for the German aircraft industry during the year 1944, since the largest proportion of the models on the assembly lines was taken up by this vast array, all in production at the same time. Further complicating production was the fact that the industry had been forced by Allied bombing to disperse its manufacturing centres, and the work of hundreds of sub-contractors involved in producing components for the aircraft had to be co-ordinated. The German war effort had finally been brought to its fullest effectiveness; moreover, despite the bombing raids, overall production rose compared to all previous years. Nevertheless, even though production increased, the growing requirement for fighter aircraft outpaced the performance of the manufacturers. A decision was made in mid-1944 to 'standardize' on a new model of the 109, the Bf 109K, by which course of action many problems would be eliminated.

K-series aircraft did not take over completely from the Gs. The end of the war found two further models of the G series added to the list, which, along with the

◄ The 'Galland hood' was a lighter, improved cockpit canopy and was standard on the Bf 109G-10 and later versions.

► A substantial number of Bf 109G-12s were built for flying schools, converted from G-1, G-5 and G-6 airframes.

◄ Bf 109 'Gustav' G-14/R3 *Werk Nr.* 413555 of *Jagdgeschwader 3 'Udet'* in 1944.

G-10, were to be seen on the assembly line at the same time as the K series until the last day of the war. The first of these was the Bf 109G-14. Its engine was either the DB 605AS, with a larger supercharger, or the DB 605Am, with the MW 50 injection system. Armament consisted of a 20mm MG 151 and two MG 131s, with provision for the addition of R1 and R6 conversion sets, and a few models received the wooden tailplane assembly to become the Bf 109G-14/U4. The second of the new models, and the last of the G series, was the Bf 109G-16. The basic differences between this and the G-14 were the powerplant, a DB 605D, and armoured radiators and oil coolers, which were R1 and R6 modifications completed on the factory assembly lines.

September 1944 saw the introduction of the Bf 109K-0 pre-production model of the K series. Exterior departures from the later G models included lengthening the airscrew spinner and raising the line of the cowling slightly. The first production models of the K, the K-2 and K-4, paralleled the construction of the K-0s, and they appeared in October 1944. Power for the pre-production models was supplied by a DB 605DB with the GM 1 booster system, but the production versions were fitted with either a DB 605DCM, with GM 1, or a DB 605ASCM. The armament fit included the 30mm MK 108 cannon in the nose, with 60 rounds of ammunition, and a pair of 15mm cannon, with 220 rounds per gun, replacing the 13mm MG 131s found in the Gs. The K-4 differed from the K-2 in having a pressurized cabin, and later models of the K-4 replaced the MK 108 cannon with an MK 103, of the same calibre but offering a superior performance. Built primarily for bomber-interception operations, the Bf 109K-6 was similar to the K-4 with the exception of

◄ A Messerschmitt Bf 109K-4/R3 of *1/JG* 77 minutes before take-off against incoming USAAF B-17s, October 1944.

◄ The pressurized cockpit of the Bf 109K-2. The 'Galland hood' was of lighter construction and provided improved vision, while the *Panzerglas* head shield gave the pilot better vision to his rear.

German Wartime Aircraft Production 1939–1945

Year	1939	1940	1941	1942	1943	1944	1945*	Grand totals
Bf 109s	449	1,693	2,764	2,665	6,247	13,786	2,969*	30,573
Total fighters	605	2,746	3,744	5,515	10,898	25,285	4,935*	53,728
Total aircraft	2,518	10,247	12,401	15,409	24,807	40,593	7,539*	113,514

* Figures only until 30 April 1945.

Note: Fighters made up approximately 47 per cent of total German aircraft production; the Bf 109 accounted for approximately 57 per cent of all fighter production and about 27 per cent of all aircraft production. The figures in the table exclude German aircraft manufactured under licence in other countries.

a pair of MK 103 or MK 108 cannon carried in gondolas under the wings and a pair of MG 131s replacing the fuselage-mounted MG 151s. Few examples of this aircraft were used operationally.

The last two models of the K series, the K-10 and K-14, were also the last of Messerschmitt's fighters to come from the assembly lines during the Second World War. The K-10 was evolved for use as a bomber-destroyer and featured two wing-mounted 15mm MG 151s, two fuselage-mounted MG 131s and the MK 103 mounted with the engine. The K-14, powered by the DB 605L, offered a greatly increased performance: it was capable of flying at about 460mph and at an operational altitude of 38,000ft. The armament was not as heavy as that of the K-10, comprising an MK 108 or MK 103 and two MG 131s in the usual location.

Final variants

As the combat ceilings for all aircraft rose during the war, Messerschmitt prepared a design to meet the requirements of a high-performance fighter. This project eventually resulted in four test aircraft, designated Bf 109 V49, V50, V54 and V55, intended to operate at over 40,000ft. The best points of each of these test aircraft were combined into the pre-production Bf 109H-0, which featured the fuselage of a Bf 109F-4/Z, a DB 601E-1 engine with GM 1, and cabin pressurization. The wings had been increased in span to slightly more than 39ft by inserting a parallel-chord centre-section, the landing gear being moved to the outer edges of this new section. With a weapons assortment of two MG 17s and single MG 151, these aircraft were tasked with investigating the problems associated with high-altitude flying. The H-1, which followed, was based on the G-5 airframe powered by a DB 605A with GM 1 booster, had an armament similar to that of the H-0, and had space available to incorporate reconnaissance camera equipment. H-1 machines were supplied to the *Luftwaffe* for operational evaluation, and a number of armed reconnaissance flights were conducted over England. The more favourable performance of Kurt Tank's Ta 152H shifted the *Luftwaffe's* attention towards that particular aircraft, however, and further development of the Bf 109H ceased.

◄ The Focke-Wulf Ta 152H heavy fighter was powered by a Junkers Jumo 213 twelve-cylinder, water-cooled engine (which was also fitted to the Ju 88G four-seat night fighter).

The most unusual design modification carried out on the 109 was the *Zwilling* version, the Bf 109Z, which combined two fuselages in one aircraft. The idea behind this undertaking was to produce a heavy fighter without disrupting established production programmes by introducing a totally new model into the line. Two Bf 109F airframes were joined by a parallel-chord centre-section and a new horizontal tail. The armament and engines (DB 601E-1s) were retained, and an ETC 250 bomb rack was placed beneath the new centre wing, the original port and starboard wing panels remaining in place on the port and starboard fuselages respectively. The pilot flew the aircraft from the left-hand cockpit, the right one being modified as an area to store fuel. A single prototype was completed, but it was damaged during a bombing raid and the project was abandoned in 1944.

The Bf 109 in Action

The Bf 109's biggest attribute was its speed – it was as fast as, or faster than, most contemporary piston-engine aircraft – but it was less manageable than most major Allied fighters. Like many thoroughbreds, it showed no mercy to a man who did not know its peculiarities, many of which were inherent in the design – notably the small vertical stabilizer and rudder and the narrow-tracked, outward-retracting main landing gear. Landing on a bumpy, grassy field was extremely dangerous, because the aircraft had a tendency to pull to one side at low speeds, while the narrow-tracked undercarriage did not provide as much stability as did the wide-tracked gear on, for example, the Focke-Wulf Fw 190, the North American P-51 Mustang and the Republic P-47 Thunderbolt. The compactness of the aircraft was also something of a liability: the 109 was all engine, pilot and fuel, with very little 'dead space', making it very vulnerable to concentrated enemy fire.

In a recent interview, ex-*Luftwaffe* pilot *Oberleutnant* Bernt Büttner told of his experiences with the Bf 109G. Büttner had spent the major part of the Second World War flying the twin-engined Messerschmitt Bf 110 and the Junkers Ju 88 dive-bomber, but switched to the Bf 109 near the end of hostilities when the need for experienced pilots reached a critical stage. The first flight was uneventful until the young *Oberleutnant* set the aircraft down for a landing at Kaufbeuren in Bavaria. As the aircraft's main gear touched the grassy field, one wheel hit a slight depression in the ground that caused the wing tip to dip. As the wheel cleared the depression, the other wing tip dropped alarmingly, and the pilot continued down the runway, rocking from side to side, until one tip made contact with the ground because of the buckling of the landing gear strut on that side of the aircraft. The wing tip dug into the ground, and the Bf 109 spun around to a complete stop. The bruises of Büttner's knees were nothing compared to the bruise to his dignity – that of a veteran pilot who had completed almost 200 operational missions. Büttner's second flight in a Bf 109G that day was much less exciting, and he even succeeded in landing the aircraft safely; before he brought the machine down, however, he seriously considered using the more direct route aided by his parachute!

Büttner was an exception. Many young student pilots were not fortunate enough to be alive to make a second flight in the Bf 109. Even the most experienced German fighter pilots had bad days when it seemed as though they had never flown a Bf 109 before; on other days, conversely, it was difficult to determine whether the man was in any way distinct from the machine, when both performed as a single entity. In knowing hands, the Bf 109 did exactly what it was designed to do: provide a stable platform for the airborne use of its cannon and heavy machine guns. When a good pilot took a Bf 109 into combat against an aircraft equal to his own, the matter was decided by the better pilot, or plain good luck; given the right circumstances, an experienced German pilot could outfly and outshoot even those opponents that tactics and technical manuals deemed impossible to defeat.

The Bf 109 could climb to 7,000m (about 23,000ft) in six minutes, and was therefore very valuable as an interceptor. The last operational versions could fly at maximum speeds of approximately 450–475mph and were armed with three extremely fast firing cannon – a lethal punch for such a small package. A crew member of a B-17F described the striking power of the Bf 109G as follows:

▶ The Bf 109G-5 had its cockpit pressurized.

▶ A head-on view of a Bf 109F, showing the wing radiators, the oil cooler located under the fuselage and the 20mm MG FF/M cannon firing through the propeller spinner.

. . . They [the Bf 109s] would pretend to come in on one of the other ships, and then do a twenty degree turn and shoot the hell out of us. Mostly they came from the rear, but at least one of them came up under us from the front, stalled and, as it fell off, racked us the length of the Fortress's belly. I could feel his hits banging into us. As a matter of fact, I could feel the effect of all their fire. It was rather like sitting in the boiler of a hot water heater and being rolled down a hill.

He went on to describe the visual effects of the attack from underneath the bomber:

Then I looked out at the right wing and saw it was shot to hell. There were holes everywhere. A lot of them were 20mm cannon holes, and they tear a hole in the skin you could shove a sheep through. The entire wing was just a bunch of holes!

A four-engined bomber could take a lot of punishment, however, and it usually required more than just one firing pass to dislodge an aircraft from its protective formation and then at least several more passes to ensure a 'kill'. Heinz Knocke, a Bf 109 pilot and commander of the 5th *Staffel* of *Jagdgeschwader II*, described one such kill in his book *Bordbuch eines Jagdfliegers*:

I zoom in for a second attack from the front. This time I open fire from a little below the bomber's flight path, and continue to fire until I have to swerve to keep from colliding with the enemy. As I dive away I look back and notice that flames are coming from the belly and rear fuselage of the big Liberator (B-24). It banks slightly to the right and then turns out of the formation. Two more times I attack from above and to the rear. Tracers from the defensive fire whip past my head, and my aircraft shakes from the recoil of my own machine guns and cannons as well as the enemy's hits. As I grip the control stick with both hands, I watch my cannon shells strike the bomber along the top of the fuselage and the right wing. As the fire spreads along the wing the right inboard engine stops and suddenly the right wing breaks completely away and the bomber goes into a vertical dive. A long tail of smoke marks the bomber's path.

▼ A series of photographs taken by a German infantryman from the trenches showing the downing of an SB-2 bomber by *Oberleutnant* Kurt Sochatzky of 7/*JG 3* 'Udet', summer 1941.

◄ **A Bf 109G zooming in for a head-on attack.**

◄ *Hauptmann* **Heinz Knocke,** *Staffelkapitän* **of 5/*JG II*, was one of the special group of '*Viermottöter*' ('four-engine-killers'). He finished the war with 33 victories, nineteen of which were four-engined bombers.**

► *Oberstleutnant* **Adolf Galland and** *Oberst* **Werner Mölders during a meeting in France, August 1940.**

The aces

The men who flew the Bf 109 were no different from the men who flew P-40s, P-51s, P-38s, Spitfires, Hurricanes or any of the other aircraft found in the air forces of the Second World War. These men shared a common bond – the love of flying, an attribute transcending policies and politics.

It is difficult to define any special characteristics peculiar to *Luftwaffe* pilots as a whole. They were men caught up in circumstances beyond their individual control but believed that they had a duty to perform. One can but admire their courage when, later during the war, the skies over their own homeland were darkened by the vast air armada of Allied bomber and fighter aircraft and they continued to fly against these overwhelming odds.

An analysis of any group of people will show that it includes those of the weakest natures and those of the strongest, and is as diversified as the total number of its members. The 109 pilots were no exception to this rule. They were not initially specialists, but through experience they did become some of the best aerial hunters the world has seen. They were drawn from all walks of life: unlike the pilots of the USAAF, the men of the 109s could be enlisted personnel as well as officers. Ability, and ability alone, counted.

The story of the men who flew and cared for the Bf 109 is the story of the German *Luftwaffe* from its birth in 1935 to its death in the spring of 1945. When Werner Mölders, one of Germany's greatest fighter pilots, flew his first combat patrol over the skies of France in early 1940, he already had fourteen air-to-air victories to his credit; all were gained during the Spanish Civil War, and all with the Messerschmitt Bf 109. Another pilot who obtained his first combat experience in the skies of Spain was Adolf Galland, later to become the commanding general of the *Luftwaffe*'s fighter arm. This accumulation of experience proved beneficial to

the German Air Force: the most successful pilots were able to recount their experiences to the high command and the training command – and especially to the Messerschmitt design team – pointing out the major faults of the Bf 109 and recommending changes, additions and modifications for future models. They were also able to pass on their knowledge to the newer pilots joining the fighter units at the fronts.

Records kept by the *Luftwaffe* show that 105 German fighter pilots, and possibly four others, were able to use Bf 109s at some time during their combat careers to score more than one hundred air-to-air victories. Two of these men each scored more than three hundred victories, and thirteen others were able to score more than two hundred each. Altogether, the 105 men were able to account for the air-to-air destruction of nearly 15,000 enemy aircraft! According to Allied practice, a pilot became an 'ace' when he had destroyed five or more enemy aircraft in the

▶ *Oberleutnant* Erich Hartmann in his Bf 109G-14, which sports his personal marking – his wife's name in a red heart pierced by Cupid's arrow – under the cockpit. Russia, summer 1944.

air, and the fragmentary German records gathered by the historical section of the *Gemeinschaft der Jagdflieger* (German Fighter Pilots' Association) in Munich show that the title 'ace' may belong to more than 2,500 German pilots. These figures are only approximate – there may be more!

How is this possible? Are the figures accurate? Is it possible that while the highest-scoring American ace, Major I. Bong, flying P-38 Lightnings, was able to bring down a total of forty Japanese aircraft in the Pacific, the highest-scoring German ace, *Major* Erich 'Bubi' Hartmann (only twenty-two years old at the end of the war), was able to shoot down no fewer than 352 enemy aircraft? Looking into the credibility of these figures, the following facts should be considered:

1. Germany was engaged in war for six years, 1939–45.
2. A pilot who was able to fly combat missions continually for a period of three years was lucky to be alive.
3. German fighters were restricted in range and endurance because of their minimal fuel capacity.

◀ Yet to become the highest scoring ace of all time, *Leutnant* Erich Hartmann stands before his Bf 109G on 2 September 1943. The striking flatness of the vast Russian Front is apparent.

How do these facts tie in with the figures mentioned? The *Luftwaffe* was engaged in actual hostilities almost continuously for six years, three more years than the American forces, who were involved in the war from 1942 to 1945. The Poles fought the Germans for a total of three months, the French fought the Germans in the air for approximately seven months, and the Russians were involved against them for four years; only the Royal Air Force was in combat for a comparable length of time. Thus the Germans had more opportunities to score their air-to-air kills simply because they were at war longer than anyone else.

A common practice among the Allies, especially the US Army Air Force, was to transfer a pilot back to the home area after he had completed an overseas tour of one hundred combat missions, which might be flown over a period of from four months to a year. The German fighter pilot, however, from 1943 onwards, was stationed at or near home. Because of the Allied bombing offensive, which meant streams of bombers over German cities day and night, he and his aircraft were neded every time there was a bombing alert. He did not fly a set number of missions then then get transferred – unless his nerves were frayed or he was so 'shot up' that he would no longer be effective as a fighter pilot.

Towards the end of the war Germany had no thorough air crew training programme, and the experienced *Luftwaffe* pilots lacked confidence in the

◄◄Blond, handsome and slender, Erich Hartmann rests atop the seat of his Bf 109G-10. His bleeding heart emblem reflects his separation from his wife Ursula, a childhood sweetheart he finally married in the summer of 1944.

◄ *Leutnant* Hans-Joachim Birkner, who flew as both Günther Rall's and Erich Hartmann's wingman, scored his first victory on 1 October 1943 and claimed his 100th Soviet aircraft on 14 October 1944. Transferred to *JG 51*, whose ninth *Staffel* he commanded, Birkner was killed on 14 December 1944 when his engine failed on take-off. At the time of his death, he had shot down 117 aircraft (including an American Mustang) in 284 missions.

◄ Four of *JG 52*'s aces cluster around *Oberstleutnant* Dietrich Hrabak's Bf 109G: (from left to right) *Oberleutnant* Friedrich Obleser (127 victories), *Leutnant* Karl Gratz (138), *Geschwader Kommandeur* Hrabak (125) and *Hauptmann* Erich Hartmann (352). All these men survived the war.

replacement pilots being sent to the combat units. The Allies, on the other hand, used the experienced pilots who had completed a combat tour to share their knowledge with the newly trained men, and a 'circle' of training and experience was thereby formed. The Germans had neither the manpower nor sufficient experienced pilots to withdraw more than a few personnel from combat flying in order to teach new recruits, and as a result German pilots flew combat missions almost from the day they were assigned to a fighter squadron until the day they were killed in action or the war ended. Moreover, during the Allied bombing offensive over Germany, *Luftwaffe* fighter pilots were not restricted as to the number of sorties they could fly, and it was not uncommon for a pilot to complete as many as five missions in one day if Allied aircraft were coming and going above his airfield.

The scoring of victories

As for the actual scoring of victories, the German Air Force had an inordinately thorough system of reports that had to be filled out when credit for an air-to-air victory was claimed. Besides the pilot's flight report, which had to include the geographical location of the air combat, the time of the action, the height of the action, and the number of cannon and machine-gun rounds expended during the action (this last was to be determined by the armourer after the aircraft had landed), a report of the action from at least one ground or air observer was required, and this had to include basically the same information as the pilot's report. In lieu of an eyewitness report, evidence of the crashed enemy aircraft, the enemy crew member's remains, or a captured crew member would suffice (and, in most cases, was preferred). Since German anti-aircraft batteries were also quite active along the front, their claims had to be separated from the air-to-air claims by

▼ *Hauptmann* Gerhard Barkhorn, wearing his Knight's Cross, is surrounded by members of his group after scoring his 250th air victory, March 1944.

◄ A toast for *Hauptmann* Barkhorn, second only to Erich Hartmann in scoring a total of 301 Eastern Front victories. He flew 1,104 missions while serving with *JG 52* from August 1940 until January 1945.

◄ The great skill and devotion of the crew chiefs of the fighter pilots was a major factor in the latter's continued effectiveness in combat.

investigation teams, and in these cases there were never more victories credited than actual physical evidence of enemy aircraft found: if, for example, twenty-six victories were claimed between a fighter group and the local anti-aircraft batteries and only fourteen wrecked enemy aircraft were found, only fourteen victories were credited. Unless there were incontrovertible evidence either way, it was a toss-up whether the victories were credited to the anti-aircraft batteries or to the fighters. The reports were submitted to the pilot's commanding officer for approval or rejection, then to the next highest man in the chain of command, until they reached the Commander-in-Chief of the *Luftwaffe*. Of course, from time to time false claims were successful in getting through the chain of command for approval, but there were also many valid claims that never got beyond the first step in the chain owing to lack of evidence, or because the enemy aircraft had fallen too far behind enemy lines to be seen by German observers in the air or on the ground.

During the war, German pilots claimed the destruction of approximately 70,000 enemy aircraft, including British, Greek, Polish, French, American, Russian, Dutch, Norwegian and Yugoslavian machines. American and British records show the loss of approximately 40,000 aircraft, and the Germans claimed only 25,000 of these. The German claims do not, therefore, seem to be out of proportion. Although the Soviet Union has, as yet, failed to publish any data, it can be assumed

► The Ilyushin Il-2 *Sturmovik* was reckoned to be the most difficult Second World War aircraft to shoot down, but some German aces mastered the art of defeating this heavily armoured Soviet ground attack machine. Here, *Luftwaffe* personnel inspect their prize.

from the yearly production figures that approximately 70,000 Soviet aircraft were destroyed by all causes. Using roughly the same ratio as between British and American losses and German claims thereof, it can be surmised that the Germans were responsible for 60 per cent of the total Soviet losses, or approximately 42,000 aeroplanes.

The attrition of German fighter aircraft and personnel, especially during the last year of the war, should not be forgotten. Total German fighter losses are estimated at about 55,000 day and night fighters – a sober assessment when one considers that the total production figures were not much more than this. German pilot losses, including those killed, missing in action and taken prisoner, amounted to more than 15,000. Although there are no adequate figures to show how many German fighter pilots were wounded or injured so severely that they could never fly again, the number must have been considerable.

Figures from the Historial Section of the German Fighter Pilots' Association, quoted in the book *Ritterkreuzträger der Luftwaffe*, by Ernst Obermaier, show that of the 564 holders of the Knight's Cross of the Iron Cross who belonged to the *Luftwaffe*'s fighter arm, 296 were killed in action or in accidents, or in some other way did not survive the war – yet these 564 men accounted for almost 36,000 aerial victories. These figures show that experience gained in combat was not enough to enable a pilot to survive the hostilities.

Rudder markings

It is not our intention to deal at length with the camouflage schemes applied to the Bf 109 during its long service life: examples of the aircraft in complete 'service dress' are shown in this book and illustrate well the basic styles and colour combinations employed on the numerous war fronts of the Third Reich, and many books devoted exclusively to the subject are readily available. Our present discussion will centre on those markings found on the rudder of the Bf 109. This small area of the aircraft's surface was the one which made each machine unique unto itself, since here was located the 'scoreboard' of aerial victories won by the pilot. The practice of keeping these tallies on the rudder appears to be a specifically German introduction, but it was not limited to fighter aircraft, and photographic evidence indicates that such scores were also kept on the rudder surfaces of bomber

aircraft to indicate the number of ships sunk, troop concentrations attacked, tanks destroyed and so forth. Other personal markings might be located on the aircraft's fuselage and ranged from coats of arms to cartoon characters (Mickey Mouse flew not only with the USAAF but with the RAF and the *Luftwaffe* as well), and included a whole range of designs, symbols and inscriptions to individual taste.

The first application of victory markings occurred three years before the outbreak of the Second World War, on the aircraft of the Condor Legion in Spain, and comprised white bars, one for each enemy plane downed. These markings were applied to the fins of the aircraft since the Spanish Nationalists' insignia, a diagonal black cross on a white background, occupied the entire rudder. However, with the return of the Legion's pilots to Germany and the opening of the Second World War, air-victory markings were placed on the rudder itself. The 109s which opened the campaign in Poland were painted overall *schwarzgrün*, or black-green (camouflage colour No. 70 from the official standards), on all upper surfaces, with *hellblau*, or light blue (No. 65), below; against this background, the markings were painted in white, with the date of the air action placed inside the bar.

The close of the Polish campaign found the fighters recamouflaged using colours 70 and 71, the latter a dark green. This scheme remained in effect until the end of 1940, at which time the colours were changed to light and dark greys, with light blue retained for all undersurfaces. Red and black bars now denoted victories, and the national identity of the downed aircraft was recorded by way of a miniature national insignia placed on or above the bar, although the sandy brown and green paintwork applied to German aircraft operating in the Mediterranean theatre led to these bars being applied in white or yellow. The later war years would find the victory markings in white, yellow, red or black (depending on the background), with or without the date and miniature insignia.

The need for the rapid identification of friendly forces during the Battle of Britain led to the introduction of temporary (washable) markings which could be changed quickly for security purposes. The areas so painted included engine cowlings, wing tips and rudders, and used a variety of different 'solid' colours. Bands around the fuselage immediately in front of the rudder assembly have been described as denoting the theatre of operation of a particular aircraft. These bands appeared towards the end of 1941, and the colour employed was often applied also to the rudder, the wing tips and portions of the cowling. In general, yellow was used for aircraft stationed on the Channel coast, in northern Europe and in northern and central Russia, and white was used for the Mediterranean and North African theatres and in southern Russia. Solid red rudders appear to have been adopted by *JG 2 'Richthofen'* at one time or another, and the choice of colour should come as no surprise. During the last year of the war other fuselage rings appeared, signifying fighter aircraft employed in the defence of the Reich. These rings were composed of two- or three-colour parallel rings, placed in the same position as the theatre bands.

During the autumn of 1940 and the Battle of Britain, a fourth *Staffel* was formed within each fighter *Gruppe*, the aircraft of one *Staffel* being equipped to act in the fighter-bomber role. To differentiate their role from the remainder of the *Gruppe*'s aircraft, the insignia of a falling bomb, solid white, was placed between the fuselage cross and tailplane. These fighter-bombers were later withdrawn from their respective *Gruppen* and formed into their own *Schnelle Kampfgeschwader* (fast-bomber squadrons) or SKGs.

As the success of individual pilots mounted, an award of the *Ritterkreuz* in one of its several grades was presented. To commemorate this event, the rudder of the pilot's aircraft would be repainted with a symbolic rendering of the award, with the number of aircraft which had been shot down to achieve this distinction placed

▶ *Oberleutnant* Hubert Mütherich (31 kills) and *Leutnant* Josef Pöhs (28) pose confidently with the former's Bf 109 after receiving Knight's Crosses, 6 August 1941. Both 5/JG 5 pilots would attain 43 victories but neither would survive the war: 'Hubs' Mütherich crashed near Leningrad the following month, and 'Joschi' Pöhs died while testing a rocket-powered Messerschmitt Me 163B Komet in December 1943.

▶▶The tally on the rudder of *Oberleutnant* Frank Liesendahl's Bf 109F flying as *Jabo* (fighter-bomber) of *10/JG 2* against British shipping, late 1941. His unit sank twenty vessels totalling 63,000 tons.

▶ The rudder of *Oberleutnant* Max Helmut Ostermann's Bf 109. The score shows his 100th victory on 12 April 1942, making him the sixth highest scorer in the *Luftwaffe*. Ostermann received the Oak Leaves after 62 victories on 10 March 1942, but he lost the contest against a Russian fighter on 9 August 1942 after scoring a total of 102.

▶▶Incredible as it may seem, over one hundred German aces each scored over one hundred aerial victories. This photograph was taken on 4 July 1943.

◄ A Bf 109F flown by Werner Mölders, *Kommandeur* of *JG 51*, shows 101 victories on its rudder. Immediately after this photograph was taken (in Russia, on 15 July 1941), Mölders was recalled to become *General der Jagdflieger* (General of Fighter Operations).

◄ The rudder of the Bf 109 flown by one of the *Luftwaffe*'s leading officers, *Hauptmann* Herbert Ihlefeld. The second from last victory recorded shows a British aircraft shot down over the Channel on 1 March 1941. Victory 32 is just being added, although the date has not been entered.

◄ *Oberfeldwebel* Stefan Litjens looks at his armourer and, on the tail of his Bf 109F, a *4/JG 53* mascot. Shortly after this photograph was taken, on 11 September 1941, the 22-victory ace was shot down by a Soviet bomber and lost an eye. Litjens overcame the handicap to fly over Malta and Tunisia, and on home defence duties. On 23 March 1944, after downing two American bombers, he injured his other eye in a belly landing, ending his 38-victory career.

above or below it. Subsequent victories were applied in the normal manner until a higher award was attained, when the process would begin once more.

There can be no doubt that the addition of these many coloured areas greatly detracted from the overall effect of the camouflage paint scheme, and from the beginning of 1942 orders were issued by the *Luftwaffe*'s Commander-in-Chief, Göring, that prominent markings were to be eliminated. However, most units ignored these instructions, even though they were issued on several occasions. A similar order prohibiting rudder victory markings was likewise ignored, this being considered a personal affront to a successful fighter pilot in any man's air force.

The Star of Africa

Hans Joachim Marseille had tremendous flying skill and a keen shooting eye. The greatest day of this young man's career came on 1 September 1942, in North Africa, when he led his squadron of Bf 109Fs as fighter escort for a group of Junkers Ju 87s as they dive-bombed British lines. The Bf 109s took off at 0730hrs and flew east to rendezvous with the dive-bombers at 0750. Covering the Stukas at an altitude of about 11,500ft, Marseille spotted a formation of ten British fighters approaching. He immediately dived to attack the American-built Curtiss P-40C Tomahawks, which were completely unaware of the German fighters. Closing to within 300ft of one British aircraft, Marseille fired one short burst with his cannon and machine guns, smashing the canopy and killing the pilot. The aircraft rolled over out of control and hurtled to the ground. The time was approximately 0820hrs. Marseille then continued after the downed pilot's wingman and fired another short burst that again struck the canopy of the British aircraft, which crashed less than a mile and a half from the first one. The time was 0821. At 0830 another British Tomahawk had spotted the Stukas and was lining up on the tail of one of the dive-bombers when Marseille fired his third short burst of the day. The cowling and wing root of the P-40C burst into long streamers of flame, and the machine dropped like a stone. It was now 0833.

A group of six Spitfires had seen the action from above and dived on Marseille's formation, firing as it came. Marseille waited until the lead Spitfire was within 400ft of his own tail before he broke sharply to the side, letting the British fighters zoom past his aircraft. As the Spitfires began their wide turn to resume combat with the Messerschmitts, Marseille pushed his throttle to the firewall, rolled his machine over, and fired at the leading aircraft at almost point-blank range. At 0839

▼ Marseille's Bf 109F takes off for another mission, Libya, March 1941.

◄◄*Leutnant* Hans Joachim Marseille, wearing the Knight's Cross he received on 22 February 1942 after scoring his 50th aerial victory. Other decorations are the German Cross in gold worn under the right pocket and the ribbon to the Iron Cross Second Class.

◄ A photograph of Marseille wearing his favourite black leather jacket and the *Luftwaffe* summer flying helmet. There is no evidence that Marseille wore goggles during his missions.

◄◄After landing, Marseille exchanged his flying helmet for the more comfortable forage cap.

◄ *Lt.* Marseille poses in his favourite flying outfit.

another column of black smoke was seen rising from the desert floor. Breaking off combat, the German fighters returned to their base to replenish their fuel and ammunition, the last one landing at 0914. Marseille's four victories had been cheap: he had expended only twenty cannon shells and sixty rounds of machine-gun ammunition.

At 1020hrs Marseille took off again to escort Stukas on a mission over the British lines, this time taking only one flight of Bf 109s with him. On the way to the rendezvous Marseille spotted two British bomber formations flying west towards the German lines, above and behind them their fighter escort. The first Tomahawks began to roll over and dive on the unsuspecting Ju 87s, but Marseille's flight met them half-way down. The P-40s immediately went into a defensive 'Lufbery circle'.* Any aeroplane caught within this circle was normally considered to be 'dead game', but Marseille charged right in and shot down a P-40 from a range of 150ft before the British could react. The British pilots were clearly stunned by the audacity of the German, but before they could break away and escape a second P-40 was absorbing a burst from Marseille's guns. These two kills came at 1055 and at 1056hrs. At the altitude at which they were flying, the P-40s were at a distinct disadvantage to the Bf 109F in terms of speed, and within two minutes Marseille had closed to within 200ft of another Tomahawk: one short burst, and the Curtiss fighter went into a glide with white smoke pouring out of his radiator. It was 1058.

Five Tomahawks were now in front of Marseille, flying in two formations of two aircraft apiece with the fifth one between them for protection. In shallow dives to gain speed on the fast-closing Messerschmitts, the British aircraft headed north towards the Mediterranean coast, but at 1101 the tail-end machine in the British formation exploded in mid-air from the impact of Marseille's cannon shells. Passing under the flaming debris, Marseille swept up behind another P-40 and fired, and the aircraft nosed over and fell. Before Marseille could do anything about the other three P-40s, another British formation was sighted flying below the Germans. Marseille seized the opportunity, dived from out of the sun and shot the tail section off one unsuspecting enemy aircraft. This last kill took place at 1105hrs.

Having missed the squadron's third mission in the early afternoon, Marseille took to the air again at 1700hrs: this time the unit was to escort twin-engined Junkers Ju 88 dive-bombers to their targets. As the bombers began to make their attacks on the British positions, about fifteen Curtiss P-40s swept in to intercept them, and, with the sun at this back, Marseille led his squadron directly through the British formation. He fired four short bursts. The first demolished a P-40 at 1745hrs; his second accounted for another one at 1746; at 1747 his third burst claimed another Tomahawk; and at 1750 his fourth tore the wing off yet another British fighter. Finally, speeding along the desert floor at altitudes of between 50 and 200ft, he manoeuvred on to the tail of another enemy fighter and shot it down at 1753hrs. With the British fighters dispersed and the Ju 88s having done their work, the German fighter squadron headed for home.

Marseille had personally destroyed seventeen British fighters that day – only one German pilot, Günter Rall, would better this score during the course of the war – and during the remainder of September he was able to account for forty-four more British aircraft. On 30 September, returning from a patrol, Marseille's Bf 109F, 'Yellow 14', began to emit smoke from the engine. The smoke began to fill the cockpit, blinding the pilot, who rolled the aircraft over on its back and jettisoned the canopy, hoping to clear the fumes. It did no good, and Marseille decided to leave. Jumping out of an aircraft is difficult enough, but Marseille's

---

* A formation named after the First World War Allied ace Raoul Lufbery.

machine was inverted, it had begun to enter a shallow dive, and it was travelling at nearly 400mph. He worked himself out of the cockpit and dropped into the rushing air, only to be struck by the vertical stabilizer of his stricken 109. His body fell to earth, his parachute unopened.

Marseille died at the age of twenty-two, on his 388th combat mission. He had shot down 158 British aircraft – a total that no other German fighter pilot would be able to match – and he had been killed by his own aircraft.

Defence of the Reich

Shortly after Marseille's death in North Africa, the Americans began to conduct their first daylight bombing raids over Europe. Since the outbreak of the Second World War, the British had carried out daylight raids, but as the American bombing effort grew, the RAF gradually switched to attacking targets during the hours of darkness. This 24-hour offensive had strategic advantages: for example, the Allies could inflict damage on the German war effort 'round the clock', forcing the German air defences to go without rest.

Perhaps the 'elite' of the German fighter pilots were those men whose duty it was to defend the air space over the territory of Germany itself. These men were the 'bomber-killers' – men whose personal skill and daring enabled them to take on, single-handedly, an entire 'box' formation of twelve four-engined bombers capable of massing a defensive firepower of 144 50-calibre machine guns, any one of which was capable of knocking a Bf 109 out of the sky. Needless to say, the majority of successful 'bomber-killers' found the law of averages catching up with them as time went on: not many of these men survived the war.

The ferocity with which the French- and Dutch-based German aircraft met the Allies left no doubt that the Germans were fighting for their lives. The hordes of machines that attacked the four-engined B-17s and B-24s made it hard for the Americans to believe that the 'Abbeville Kids', German Fighter Wings 2 and 26, were the only German aircraft in the skies over France. The *Luftwaffe*'s determination to press home the attacks made American formation flying, normally a gruelling operation, even more demanding, and each mission for Allied bomber crews was a nerve-racking, physically exhausting experience that often

▶ **Messerschmitt Bf 109Gs of *JG 50* stationed at Wiesbaden, summer 1943.**

▼ **A Bf 109F-4/Trop of *3/JG 27* prepares to taxi. The mechanic walking back carries the inertial starter crank with which he has just turned the fighter's Daimler-Benz engine.**

lasted eight or more hours. The pilots of the bombers, trying to keep in a close protective formation and to avoid the oncoming enemy fighters and anti-aircraft artillery bursts, continually had to wrench their steering columns around. They were constantly moving forward and retarding the big throttle knobs of the four engines; keeping their eyes on the multitude of gauges and instruments in front of them, to their sides and above them; checking their own position in relation to the rest of their formation; and watching the skies for the enemy. The gunners and other crewmen had an opportunity to relax occasionally during a mission, but when the German fighters came in to attack everyone with a gun at his disposal went to work, filling the skies with deadly steel, in the hope that a German fighter would fly through it before it could let loose its own ammunition in return. During such attacks the interiors of the bombers would be filled with smoke from the firing machine guns or, frequently, from fires started by German incendiary ammunition: ever present were the smells of smoke, cordite, ozone and sweat.

▶ An entire *Staffel* in flight is an impressive sight! Red rear fuselage bands and underwing 30mm cannon pods identify these Bf 109Gs as bomber-hunting *Reichsverteidigung* (Home Defence) interceptors.

For the first American airmen taking to the skies over Europe in late 1942 and early 1943, the chances of surviving twenty-five combat missions were very low, and those men who were able to survive the number of missions that made up a tour were seldom willing to stay for more. As the Americans gained combat experience, they put more bombers into the air so that more damage could be done to German ground targets: during the height of the offensive there were times when an American bomber would leave the ground every half minute from 5.30am until 2.00pm on missions over the European continent. A common tactic was to fly several groups of bombers on the same compass heading until they reached a certain point, where they would divide and then continue on their way to individual, separate targets. Thus they could attack a number of different targets at the same time, dividing and lessening the number of German aircraft that would come up to try to stop them.

Things were not made easier for the Germans when the Allies began to employ shuttle missions, flying from Britain to targets over Germany and then continuing on to the Soviet Union to land instead of returning to their British home bases. As the war progressed and suitable airfields became available to the Allies, shuttle missions were also employed from Britain over the Alps to Italy, and from Italy to the Soviet Union. These air attacks from the north-west, north, east and south divided the German air defence forces so greatly that certain German fighter groups, such as *Jagdgeschwader 3 'Udet'* and *Jagdgeschwader 27 'Afrika'*, were used as 'firemen', rushing from front to front to give their support in trying to stem the tide of Allied bombers that crossed the ever-shrinking boundaries of the German homeland. The attrition rate for German men and aircraft became so great that some fighter wings lost more than three times the complement of pilots assigned to them at the beginning of hostilities, and more than five times their original complement of aircraft.

▲ A Bf 109G-4 ready for intercepting incoming bombers.
▲▶The *Gruppen-kommandeur*'s Bf 109G-6/R6, *JG 27*.

▶ A Messerschmitt Bf 109G-5/Trop of *JG 3 'Udet'* fitted with 21cm BR 'Nebelwerfer' 42.

Throughout the bombing offensive, the Messerschmitt BF 109 variants were used mainly as high-altitude interceptors because of their high speed and rapid rate of climb. The more heavily armed Focke-Wulf Fw 190 was used as a bomber-destroyer, the Bf 109s above them engaging the Allied fighter escorts and the highest-flying bomber formations, enabling the Fw 190s to do their work more comfortably.

Responding to a raid

There are many well-written, thrilling accounts of the Allied bomber offensive as seen from the American and British points of view, notably Bert Stiles' *Serenade to the Big Bird* and Bierne Lay's *Twelve o'Clock High*, but there have been few accounts of the air war published in English from the German point of view. This is unfortunate for the interested reader who does not have a good understanding of the German language. We have alluded to the hardships faced by the German fighter pilots during the course of the war, but what was it really like? How did they live? What did they do? Why did they continue to resist when it seemed that all was lost? Enough information is available to allow the historian to piece together the ground experience of a daylight bombing raid toward the height of the air offensive. A day could have started like this:

At 0730hrs a *Luftwaffe* radar operator picks up a telephone in his bunker on the Channel coast and asks the switchboard operator for *Jagdführer Holland* (Director for Fighter Operations for Holland). He informs the *Jagdführer* that he has picked up unidentified aircraft flying toward the Dutch coast; the aircraft are multi-engined, he thinks. With this, he hangs up the telephone and goes back to his radar set.* About ten minues later, the phone rings again in the *Jagdführer*'s underground bunker, and a sound-location site on the coast reports hearing many aircraft approaching from England. This time the *Jagdführer* goes to work in earnest. Picking up a telephone, he calls all the other *Jagdführer* within a 300-mile radius and informs them of a possible air raid. Soon, optical sightings begin to come in over the telephone and radio network, giving the approximate height and direction of flight of the enemy aircraft. A raid is on the way! With five or six other fighter directors, *Jagdführer Holland* is responsible for the daytime fighter air defence of a sector of the Channel coast, and the aerial approaches to Germany. He must act very quickly now. Calling the other fighter directors in his vicinity, he passes the following message: '*Achtung! Achtung! Dicke Autos in Dora Bertha 10!*' – 'Heavy bombers now in map sector D-B-10'. It is now 0745hrs and the Allied aircraft are due to cross the coastline in another ten minutes. The fighter directors send out alerts to the fighter squadrons in their areas of responsibility; at the same time, they plot the enemy's course on a large map table, attempting to ascertain the probable targets within their areas.

It is the fighter director's duty to know what targets there are in his area, and what kind of aircraft are approaching. Knowing the aircraft type, he can guess the enemy's probable bomb load, and from the incoming reports he can plot the speed and course. The *Jagdführer* knows a lot, but perhaps he would most like to know how to stop the attack in the few minutes left before the enemy bombers pass into his sector of responsibility. During this time, the director's staff is relaying its incoming reports to staff members of the other *Jagdführer* in Denmark, northern Germany, north-west Germany and France. Now reports of other sightings of formations of enemy aircraft begin to reach *Jagdführer Holland* from the other *Jagdführer* on his network: aircraft are approaching the coast from the north-west, north and north-east.

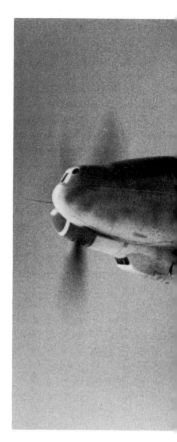

▲ A Messerschmitt Bf 110G-2 with twin 21cm Nebelwerfer 42, employed as a *Pulkzerstörer* with great effect against day bombers.
▶ A Bf 109F-5, equipped with a 66-gallon drop tank and with its engine-mounted guns removed, operating as a tactical reconnaissance aircraft.

---

*German radar sets of the time could only show objects, and the approximate bearings of these objects from the radar site, but not their altitude.

67

The problem is to discover where the Allies' targets lie, and to determine whether the bombers can be intercepted before they reach those targets. Calling the fighter units in his area, the director alerts them for take-off in twenty minutes. The fighter units are scattered in woods and fields all over the area, dispersed into groups as small as four or five aircraft to one landing field. In ten minutes the director will call again, giving them a ten-minute warning. He will issue these warnings down to the narrowest margin of time, for he knows that the fighters have severe fuel limitations and will be able to stay in the air for only about an hour under combat conditions. It is best to have the first of the defending aircraft within shooting range of the enemy when they reach the bomber stream's altitude so that they do not burn up precious fuel waiting for, or chasing after, the bombers. The fighter director also has to consider how many Allied bombers are coming. Should he allow all his available forces to take to the air at once, or should he hold some in reserve in case the Allies split up in order to pursue individual objectives? He also has to consider whether or not there will be more bombers coming as soon as the present groups have passed over.

One thing he does not have to worry about is the anti-aircraft (flak) forces assigned to his sector: the men of the *Luftwaffe*'s *Flakkorps* and the Navy's coastal anti-aircraft artillery units are already training their guns on their assigned sectors of defence – the huge chunks of air through which the bombers will have to fly. The fighter director knows that the all-purpose 88mm guns are deadly up to an altitude of 30,000ft, and if they cannot do the job, there are 105mm anti-aircraft guns, and 128mm and 150mm special-purpose guns, that can handle targets flying as high as 40,000ft.

Around the scattered airfields, pilots are already sitting in the cockpits of their Bf 109s and Fw 190s, waiting to start their engines, but not wanting to until the very last minute in order to conserve their fuel for combat. Then the pilots' earphones

► The 12.8cm *Flakzwilling* 4 (twin) could fire twenty rounds per minute up to 42,000ft against the bomber stream. The gun was loaded automatically and was employed around Germany's major cities.

◄◄An 8.8cm *Flak 36* anti-aircraft gun in a dugout, awaiting the order to fire at the approaching bombers.

◄ Railway guns could be moved to threatened target areas and support the local air defence with their firepower.

ring with the excited voice of a female radio operator in the fighter director's bunker: '*Achtung! Dicke Autos jetzt in Hanni 8000 in Anflug auf Quadrat Dora Gustav. Sind begleitet von Indianern. Achten Sie auf Indianer. Ende*' – 'Heavy bombers at 8,000 metres' altitude nearing the coast . . . . . Watch out for the Allied escort fighters.'

The pilot of the Bf 109 signals the ground crew and two greasy, black-suited men leap on to the starboard wing and grab the large handle of the magneto crank. Slowly they turn it, and a low moan is heard, growing into an ear-splitting whine as the crank turns faster and faster. The pilot turns on the ignition switch in the cockpit and the airscrew's paddle-like blades begin to turn jerkily, as spark plugs ignite the first few cylinders full of gas. Sharp pops and mechanical thumps can be heard all through the trees under which the Bf 109s are dispersed. Black clouds of smoke shoot out of the exhaust pipes, blowing back past the open canopy, and then the engine begins to roar into life as the smoke disappears. The crew chief makes one final check of the pilot's safety harness, parachute straps and oxygen connections, reaches up, and closes the canopy over the pilot's head. The ground crewmen standing behind and to the sides of the aeroplane crouch and turn their backs to the hurricane of air from the propeller. The chocks holding the landing gear in place are pulled away, and the Bf 109 moves out from the cover of the trees, its propeller blast blowing the leaves from their branches. As if controlled by one mind, five 109s roar across the grassy field and in a ragged line-abreast formation lift off the ground together, the landing-gear legs folding clumsily up into their underwing receptacles. Climbing steeply, they fly towards an imaginary point in the sky some 27,000ft overhead. These days a man has to fly extremely high to reach hell.

Within ten minutes the German fighters make contact with the enemy bombers and their fighter escort. In the *Jagdführer*'s underground bunker, radio receivers tuned to the fighters' frequencies pick up jumbled static and the muffled shouts of the pilots as they sweep in for head-on attacks: '*Horrido! Pauke, Pauke. Da sind Sie! Von Vorn! Vorsicht! Vorsicht!*'. The moments drag by in the underground plotting room as uniformed girls move symbols around on the large charts showing the positions of the enemy formations and the projected course of the bomber stream. The fighter director is hoping that the bombers will be looking for targets outside his area, but only time can tell.

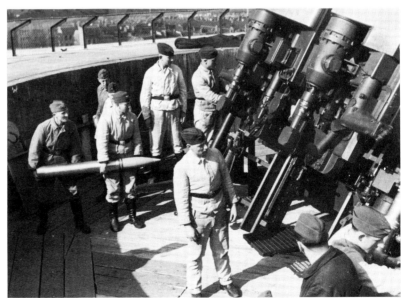

◄ A Messerschmitt Bf 109G-10 about to take off.

◄ A Bf 109G ready to meet an enemy bomber. The 66 Imp. gallon drop tank allowed the fighter to go to the target without wasting the internal fuel that was needed to enable it to spend the maximum amount of time in the vicinity of its quarry.

◄ A *Schwarm* of Bf 109s flying into action: *JG 53*, Russia, 1943.

▲ A *Kette* of *JG 53 'Pik As'* Bf 109Gs heading towards Eighth Air Force B-17 and B-24 bombers, approaching at 7,000m (21,000ft).

Outside the bunker, on ground level, the flak guns open up with their first salvos, and rolling, popping thunder can be heard over the landscape. Another sound can also be distinctly heard above the thunder of the anti-aircraft guns: from 25,000ft, it is distorted, but it grows from the thrumming of a huge horde of locusts in the distance into the rumble of an earthquake. The sound waves from hundreds of engines travel down to ground level and strike the crust of the earth, rattling windows, shaking dishes and silverware on uncleared breakfast tables, and making chandeliers tinkle and swing back and forth. If this terrible sound were all that the people looking up to the sky had to bear, things would not be so bad, but there is more to come, and everyone knows it. Up in the sky, slowly moving, ever-widening vapour trails with tiny silver dots at the point of each can be seen, looking as if a huge invisible hand were dragging scores of pencils aimlessly across the heavens. The trails intertwine gracefully, some curving around in giant swirls, others continuing on in a straight line. The bombers are directly overhead now, and the sky is filled with the stationary powder puffs of bursting anti-aircraft shells. The silver aircraft fly on, heedless of anything in their path.

The attack
An entirely different world exists at 27,000ft. The German fighters string out side by side with about half a mile of distance between them as they close to attack. The formation the German fighters have adopted affords them much more protection than one would imagine: spreading out like this makes the Allied gunners pick their targets more carefully. The fighters come in to attack. At this altitude bare flesh on any metal object will freeze immediately, but the pilots are not cold. Within the electrically heated, high-altitude flight suits in which they are encased, sweat soaks through underwear, painfully chafing armpits and crotches with each movement. The bravest fighter pilots hold their fire until their targets fill up the entire windshield. From the Allied bombers the German fighters appear as dark streaks zipping toward them. The fighters open fire, dark streaks lighting up like high-intensity strobe lights as shells spout forth from their cannon, and bright yellow and pink flaming globes from tracer ammunition float past the bombers or are absorbed by them. The forward fire of the American bombers, formerly weak, is now quite strong, and between four and six guns from each bomber can be brought to bear on the enemy attacking from the front. The fighters are travelling at approximately 400mph, while the bombers hold their formation positions as a

◄ The drop tank would be jettisoned as soon as contact was made, and the 109s could make full use of their limited, 55-minute endurance.

► The thumb on the trigger firing both the MG and cannon. The button ahead of the index finger selected the MG; that selecting the cannon is covered by the other fingers.

speed of about 200mph; the 600mph closing speed does not give much time for either party to get off a very good shot – only a few seconds pass between the time that a fighter is in shooting range until it is through the bomber formation and out of range again.

Flying in wide-turning climbs, the fighters resume their positions in front of the bombers for another attack. Again and again they come, for it is almost impossible to knock one of these big aircraft out of the sky in just a single attack: the best thing for the Germans is to wound one of the giants so seriously that it cannot maintain its position in the defensive formation and so must drop out and try to return home in its damaged condition. Away from the guns of the other Fortresses or Liberators, the bomber is a sitting duck, and the German fighters can pounce on it like jackals, tearing it to shreds, so that the bomb load will never fall on its target. Such a sight is terrible for an Allied airman to witness, but to break formation to aid a stricken bomber is a court-martial offence. Such a move is tantamount to desertion, for anyone doing so would be deserting the very forces depending upon him for a share of the mutual defence. The bomber crew members will not know

▼ A total of 3,093 B-17 bombers were lost between August 1942 and May 1945.

how many of their squadron friends are alive until they land after the mission is over. The ground crews of missing aircraft will stare in disbelief: they will probably never see the men and machines they worked with again.

On the ground, in the anti-aircraft artillery pits, the gun crews have found the altitude of the bombers and are firing as fast as their guns will permit. Earlier, they had searched for the correct height by firing shells with charges of differing power – as each shell exploded in the air, it gave off a coloured smoke. Between 20,000 and 30,000ft the sky was filled with purple, white, yellow, pink, orange and black bursts, but now only black and white bursts, like so much cotton wool, dot the sky between, below and above the enemy formations. The flak crews' object is not so much to shoot down a particular enemy aircraft as to fill the sky so full of exploding steel that some plane will certainly fly through it and be hit. For this reason, each battery of guns is assigned a certain plot of sky to keep filled with shells.

Once the flak barrage begins in earnest, the *Luftwaffe* fighters try to stay away from the bursting shells and concentrate on other bombers which have not yet reached the anti-aircraft fire. The discomfort caused by the bursting flak and flying shrapnel, as well as by the German fighter attacks, shows on the bomber formations. They rock, jink, slowly spread out, then speed up again to close the formation as more fighters come in. The waist gunners in the bombers shout, turn their heavy gun mounts towards the enemy, fire out short bursts, stumble on expended shell casings that litter the floor of the fuselage, struggling in their flying suits like huge grizzly bears, fight for balance as the bombers jerk and rock from evasive action or from the concussion of bursting flak shells, and try to concentrate on the next oncoming German. The speed of the aerial attacks, and the sheer number of aircraft, makes it virtually impossible to fire at every single German that comes within range, and the gunners have to be content with shooting at every

▼ **A Bf 109G of *JG 3* '*Udet*' is prepared for a long-range intercept mission.**

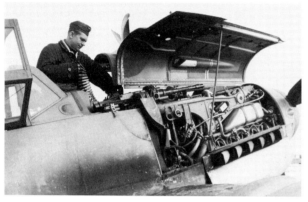

third or fourth, as they attack from above, below, the sides, the front and the rear of the formation.

The German fighter pilots, drenched in their own sweat and with muscles aching from the forces of high-gravity manoeuvres, continually swivel their heads, always on the lookout for attacking Allied fighters. In for another attack at a smoking Fortress, this time from above and to the side. Watch the instruments. Watch the target. Watch the gun sight. Watch out for enemy fighters. Come from the sun so the bomber's gunners can't see you until it's too late to shoot accurately. Give them the smallest, least-vulnerable target possible. Now the bomber fills the sight. Push the cannon and machine-gun firing buttons on the control stick. Feel the fighter rattle and shake from the firepower. Here come the bright yellow streaks of the tracers from the enemy. See the pink and black explosions of the cannon shells on the enemy bomber. '*Pauke! Pauke!*'* Now, roll over so all he can shoot at is your armoured belly and get the hell out of this mess. Stick over the back . . . More rudder. Tighten the muscles. Watch the instruments. Where are the enemy fighters? Instruments . . . Fuel! Almost all gone . . . Just enough to make it back. If a Mustang or a Typhoon gets me now, I can't fight back. Ammo gone . . . gas gone. Ears ache, arms hurt, headache from too much squinting. Neck almost numb from turning. Stomach aches. Feet cold. Wish I was back in bed. *Sakrament!* I'm tired.

The German fighter pilot has to get his machine back down to the ground from 20,000ft. When he reaches his base, he must get it under cover fast, for Allied fighter-bombers fly around looking for German aircraft on the ground. Even before the propeller stops spinning, ground crewmen rush out and manhandle the

---

*A hit scored on an enemy aircraft (literally, a drum beat).

◄◄ Filling the oxygen
bottles for the respirator
of a Bf 109K.
◄ The Bf 109E's
armament consisted of
two 7.92mm MG 17
machine guns in the
fuselage (1,000 rounds
per gun) and two wing-
mounted 20mm MG FF/
M cannon (60).

◄◄ Each of the
ammunition canisters for
the twin engine-mounted
13mm MG 131 machine
guns of the Bf 109G held
300 rounds.
◄ Belts of 15mm and
7.92mm ammunition for
the guns of a Bf 109F.

aircraft under the cover of trees and camouflage netting. Before the pilot's safety harness is unhooked, the armourers have opened the gun bays and are busy replacing spent ammunition; later, the barrels will be swabbed out and cleaned, and the CO_2 bottles of the gun-cocking devices will be refilled. Sheet-metal workers are busy popping rivets off panels with battle damage so that they may be replaced. The cowling is removed and the engine mechanics are checking and adjusting anything that is not too hot to handle. The pilot pulls his tired body out of the cockpit, stands on the wing root for a minute inhaling the forest air, then gets down from the wing and walks towards the operations shed on legs still shaking from the excitement of combat and the nearness of death.

The refuelling crew now goes to work on the aircraft, and the squadron's technical officer and inspection team go over it from stem to stern, checking for unseen damage: this 109 has to fly again as soon as the ground crew is finished. In the operations shed, the pilot slumps into a chair and begins to fill out his mission report, giving details of the type and number of aircraft he engaged, whether he did any damage to them, and who might have witnessed his actions. The day is not over yet.

As more and more Allied bombers fill the sky overhead, and as his fighters are still being re-armed and refuelled, the *Jagdführer* asks the neighbouring fighter directors for help from their unused squadrons, but the answers are short and to the point. Some of the Allied bombers have separated from the main group and are heading in other directions, and all possible aircraft that can be flown for defensive purposes have already been committed to battle. By noon those pilots who rose to face the enemy bombers early that morning have already flown two missions against the bomber stream and are landing. The last squadrons of four-engined bombers are now overhead, flying towards the heartland of Germany.

The tired pilots will now have a chance to get a little rest, eat some hot food, and maybe change their sweaty clothes. As the bombers pass, the sky grows quiet again. All that is heard is the rustle of the wind through the leaves of the trees and the clanking of metal on metal as the greasy mechanics work on their charges for the third time this day.

Turnaround time

The *Jagdführer* in Holland, north-west Germany and northern Germany, having been forced to meet almost four hours of continual aerial attack during the morning, now sit down to determine their losses in men and material; their gains are also counted. Special teams are sent out to comb the wrecks of aircraft for the dead and, if possible, their identification. Allied wrecks are searched for any new equipment of intelligence value such as bomb sights and radar gear. Since captured Allied airmen are the *Luftwaffe*'s responsibility, the fighter director must also co-ordinate with other teams searching for the lucky men able to reach the ground safely by parachute. Perhaps the greatest concern of the *Jagdführer* now is what he will do this afternoon: if the bombers take the same route back to Britain, he will have to commit his forces to action again. No time is wasted in informing the various units under his command what is expected of them and in what state of readiness they must remain.

The flak gunners have already begun to clear their pits of the piles of heavy, brass, empty shell casings fired during the morning's action, and others are swabbing out the barrels of their guns. Each time one of these heavy guns is fired, the recoil caused by the exploding, expanding gases of the powder charge exerts tremendous forces on the recuperator mechanisms and cradles of the gun mount. Every bolt and nut that can be seen and reached by human hand must be checked for play and tightened down again. A careful inspection of each gun is made so that the weapon can keep its accuracy until the barrel needs changing. Men who have carried heavy shells all morning from the ammunition storage bunkers to the gun pits must now redouble their efforts to empty the pits of expended casings and replenish the guns with new ammunition before the next bombers are sighted. Food and rest come second to the duty before them.

The mechanics at the airfields are working as fast as they can. Some aircraft require new engines, so they shove and curse to get the powerplants from their special handling dollies to the engine mounts on the aircraft. Stripped to the waist, drenched in sweat and covered with grease and oil, they bolt the engines to the mounts, then busy themselves with hooking up the electrical conduits and fuel and oil lines. Cannon barrels are changed and the guns are bore-sighted and test-fired. Pilots scheduled to fly the next mission are already in their aircraft for their *Sitzbereitschaft*, or cockpit readiness. They read, talk to ground crewmen, or just stare at the surroundings, but all ears are tuned to the sound of the static on the radio, and the girl's voice that may come out of it any second with a warning of approaching enemy aircraft. Some of the pilots who did not return in their aircraft from the morning flights are arriving now with their parachutes wrapped in huge bundles under their arms, occasionally stumbling on the nylon risers that drag on the ground. These men will not be flying the same aircraft again – some of them wish that they will *never* have to fly an aircraft again – but each is aware that if, out of this multitude of enemy bombers, only one is destroyed before it is able to drop its bomb load on German soil, many lives will be saved.

▼ *Major* Brändle looks on while two mechanics examine damage to the DB 605 powerplant of his Bf 109G.

Defending the Reich is as tiring as it is dangerous. Many of the men in the *Jagdführer*'s bunker, in the anti-aircraft gun pits and on the airfields will be directly affected by the bombing in Germany this day. Some will lose their homes, others their parents; still others will lose their families, and some will lose everything. Unfortunately for the pilots, the war will still go on this afternoon whether they fly again or not. There will still be tomorrow for flying, and, for the very lucky ones, the day after as well.

Finale

After 1943 German fighter-pilot losses became unbearable. There were never enough new men to replace those who had fallen, and these losses led ultimately to the complete destruction of the fighter arm. Perhaps the most effective mission flown by the German fighter arm in the late years of the war was the one that took place 1 January 1945 under the code-name Operation *'Bodenplatte'*, in which about 800 German fighters of all types participated in an all-out attack against Allied airfields in France and the Benelux countries and some 250 Allied aircraft of all types were destroyed on the ground and in the air.

This was the last big mission flown by the German Air Force. With the Allied bombers concentrating on German fuel sources, the last few reserves were either destroyed or else turned over to the units that were operating jet aircraft, but an exception was *'Rammkommando Elbe'*, equipped mostly with the Bf 109. This was a group of volunteer pilots, most with only one or two flights to their credit, whose

▼ **A Bf 109F of *II/JG 54*, flown by the *Gruppen-Adjutant*, is rigged in flying position to enable the guns to be aligned.**

mission it was to fly their aircraft into Allied bombers and, using their propellers as giant circular saws, rip off rudders, wings or any other parts of the bombers they could get close to. On 7 April 1945 approximately 120 aircraft in four groups took to the air to attack an Allied bomber formation.

Production of the Bf 109 ceased in Germany at the end of the Second World War, but continued in Czechoslovakia after the re-emergence of that country as an independent nation. Although the aircraft was no longer officially called the Messerschmitt Bf 109, it remained so to all who knew it. A number of these entered service with the Czechs, who also sold some to Israel for use in her 1948 campaign against the Arab states. Czech versions of the Bf 109 continued flying until about 1957, when the last one was scrapped.

Strangely enough, the one country that operated the Messerschmitt Bf 109 longer than any other was Spain. The Spanish Nationalist Air Force took delivery of their first Bf 109 (a 109B of the Condor Legion) in March 1937, and about 100 Bf 109s of various types were shipped to Spain between the years 1937 and 1945. After the war the engines of the 25 Bf 109Gs remaining in Spanish service were changed from the reliable but out-of-production DB 605 to the Hispano-Suiza 12-Z-89 of approximately the same horsepower, while later variants were fitted with the Rolls-Royce Merlin, which also powered the 109's one-time mortal enemy, the North American P-51 Mustang. As late as the summer of 1962, the writer saw four of these Spanish-built Bf 109s (or HA1112-M1Ls as they were called by the Spanish) take off on a flight from Getafe Air Field near Madrid. The HA1112 is no longer listed on the inventory of the Spanish Air Force, but four of the aircraft that remained in flying condition were sold in 1967 to members of the Confederate Air Force of Harlingen, Texas, where they may be seen each autumn in a mock-combat flying display with other famous fighters of the Second World War.

▲ Attrition in the German fighter force was high while it was defending the Reich against the combined strength of the RAF and USAAF fighter and bomber armadas.

Photo Gallery

▶ Seventeen-plus Bf 109Cs of *1/JG 137* at Sondhofen at the dawn of the Second World War.

▶ Flying activities at Sondhofen, summer 1938. Most accidents involving student pilots occurred during this type of manoeuvre owing to the narrow-tracked landing gear of the Messerschmitt fighter.

▶ Landing on unimproved fields such as that shown in this photograph had to be practised over and over again, and the experience was well appreciated two years later on all fronts.

◄ Map reading – a very important part of the prewar *Luftwaffe*'s excellent pilot training.

► An armourer working on the MG 17 pack of the Bf 109C. The access panel for the wing-mounted MG 15 is open for servicing.

► 'Red 12' and '5' of *II Gruppe/Jagdgeschwader 51* (later *'Mölders'*) on take-off.

◄ The two engine-mounted MG 17s of the early Bf 109 types fired 7.92mm infantry ammunition, which was also used by the Army for the 98 K carbine and MG 34 machine gun.

► A Bf 109E-1 of *Gruppenkommandeur IV Gruppe/JG 132*, spring 1939. The aircraft in the background is that of the *Gruppen* adjutant.

▲ Mechanics of *JG 53 'Pik As'* taking a short rest in front of a Bf 109E. A Junkers Ju 52 transport is seen in the background. Summer 1941.

◄ Messerschmitt Bf 109 fuselages are seen under construction in this factory photograph taken at the Augsburg plant, Bavaria, in 1940.

▲ Extensive sub-contracting and a lack of skilled labour took its toll in terms of the quality of construction work as the war progressed. German engineers therefore resorted to looser tolerances, self-aligning bushings, hand-fitted fillets and body putty in the maufacture of Bf 109s and other *Luftwaffe* aircraft.

◄ Bf 109Gs in various stages of assembly. Prefabricated parts of the aeroplane came from the various small sub-contractors throughout Germany and occupied Europe to be assembled in record time.

◄ Some 33,000 Bf 109s were built, making it the second most widely produced military aircraft in history after the Ilyushin *Sturmovik*. Bf 109Gs are shown here undergoing final assembly on parallel lines.

▼ The highest production rate of new aircraft was achieved in 1944, the year of the heaviest bomber raids, when a grand total of 14,000 Bf 109s left the factories.

► Bf 109Gs during assembly in a factory in Germany.

85

◄▲Factory workers apply national insignia to the wing of a Bf 109 – white on the black of the *Balkenkreuz*.

◄◄The masked-off spinner of a Bf 109F receives its colours from an airbrush.

▲ A new Bf 109G receives a unit marking on special camouflage in the field.

◄ The windshield of a Bf 109E is carefully cleaned by its ground crew. Evident in the well-appointed cockpit are the Revi reflecting gun sight and the flare pistol (right).

► The cockpit of the Bf 109 was cramped but functional, with all the instruments well placed.
▼ The cockpit interior of a Bf 109G-6, the Revi C/12D reflector gun sight visible at top right. The pilot was protected by the 90mm armour of the laminated windscreen.

▲ The shoulder harness and the crank stowed over the methonol/water tank are evident in this photograph.

◄ The pilot would sit on his chute, which fitted into the *Wanne* (tub) of the seat. To his left were the emergency handwheel for lowering the undercarriage and the tailplane trim adjustment wheel.

► The pilot's view as he entered the Bf 109 cockpit. compact, and filled with instruments and controls.

◄ A young 109 pilot poses with his mascot. This Bf 109E has curved, 6mm armour plate over the pilot's head.
▼ Hans Joachim Marseille in the cockpit of his Bf 109F-4/Trop. The yellow triangle indicates 87-octane grade fuel, although 92-octane was generally used by the *Luftwaffe*.
► *Oberleutnant* Erich Hartmann.

▲ *Oberleutnant* Hans-Ekkehard Bob posing with a scoreboard of nineteen victories on 7 March 1941 after receiving his Knight's Cross flying with *III/JG 54*.

◄ *Leutnant* Franz Schiess poses with his Bf 109F at Biala-Zerbow, USSR, in the summer of 1941. The first of his 67 victories – five fighters and nine bombers – are indicated on the rudder. Schiess was reported missing in action on 2 September 1943 after an encounter with Allied fighters in the Mediterranean theatre.

◄▲ A Bf 109C of *8 Staffel/ JG 51 'Mölders'*, 1938.
▲ A Bf 109E of *1/JG 137 'Barnberger Reiter'*.
◄ A Bf 109E of *4 Staffel/ JG 53 'Pik As'* flown by *Lt.* H. Kroeck, 1939.
►▲ A Bf 109E of *Jagdfliegerschule 2* (Flying School 2).
► Pilots of the 3rd *Staffel, Lehr-Geschwader 2* (Training Squadron 2) painted Mickey Mouse with an umbrella and shovel on their sky-blue Bf 109Es. France, May 1940.

Hier
anheben

WF

Hier
aufbocken

W. Nr.

◄ A Bf 109F-2 of *III/JG 2 'Richthofen'*, 1941.
◄▼A Bf 109E of *9 Staffel/ JG 26 'Schlageter'*.
► One of *III Gruppe/JG 27*'s Bf 109Es.
▼ A Bf 109E of *II Gruppe/JG 51 'Mölders'*, 1940.
▼►An *8 Staffel/JG 54 'Grünberz'* Bf 109E.

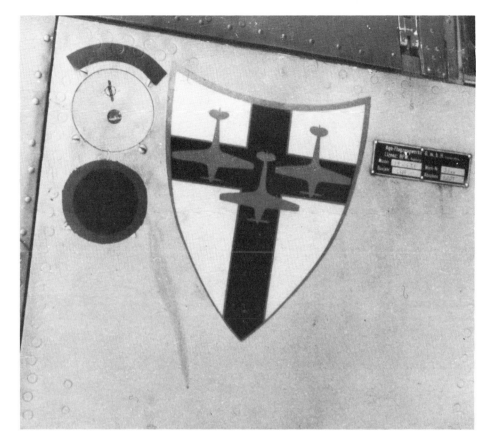

► A Bf 109E of *II Gruppe/JG 54 'Grünherz'*.
▼ The scoreboard of *Oberleutnant* Erich Schmidt's Bf 109F-2, here having victory number 24 added to the tally, eventually recorded 47 aerial 'kills'.

▲ A Bf 109F/Trop of *I Gruppe/JG 27*.

► *Major* Galland in the cockpit of his Bf 109E during the height of the Battle of Britain. The aircraft sports his famous personal emblem – Mickey Mouse with cigar, axe and pistol.

▲ A Messerschmitt Bf 109E-7/B photographed during the Balkan campaign, summer 1940.

▶▲Pilots of *JG 53 'Pik As'* pose with *Oberleutnant* Erich Schmidt, wearing his newly awarded Knight's Cross, during the Battle of Britain. Schmidt flew with *III/JG 53*, scoring his first victory on 18 August 1941, and was killed by Russian flak on 31 August 1942. His total score was 47 enemy aircraft, eighteen of which were British.

▶ Messerschmitt Bf 109E-4s of *Jagdgeschwader 53* based at Dinan, France, August 1940.

◄ Dressed for conditions in North Africa during the summer of 1941, a ground crew member touches up the lion's head insignia of *1/JG 27* on the yellow cowl of this Messerschmitt Bf 109E-4/N Trop.

▼ A *JG 53 'Pik As'* Bf 109E-4 fighter flying escort for Heinkel He 111s of *Kampfgeschwader 53*.

► The Bf 109E-4 of *Major* Helmut Wick, *Gruppenkommandeur* of *1/JG 2 'Richthofen'*, based at Beaumot-le-Roger, France, in September 1940.

►▼ Helmut Wick was one of the top-scoring aces during the Battle of Britain, ranking alongside Adolf Galland and Werner Mölders.

◄ *Oberleutnant* Wick graphically describing his latest encounter over the British Isles. The bomber life-vest he is wearing is unusual attire. Wick was shot down over the Isle of Wight on 28 November 1940 and parachuted into the Channel; his score was 56 in the West.

▼ *Hauptmann* Werner Mölders, *Kommodore* of *JG 51 'Mölders'*, in the cockpit of his Bf 109E-4.

► Werner Mölders (now *Major*), in company with members of *JG 51*, describes his 49th and 50th victories to *Generalmajor* Theo Osterkamp (left), *Jafü* of the English Channel sector and First World War ace with 32 victories (plus six in the Second World War).

► Rudder markings on Werner Mölders' Messerschmitt Bf 109E show 54 victories. Germany's first great ace of the Second World War, Mölders broke the 'Red Baron's' First World War record of 80 victories and was the first fighter pilot to be decorated with the Knight's Cross after 25 victories. He was shot down near Compiegne and taken prisoner, but subsequently he became *Kommodore* of *JG 51* in the English Channel sector on 27 February 1940. He was transferred with his Wing to the Eastern Front on 10 June 1941, at which time his score in the West stood at 68.

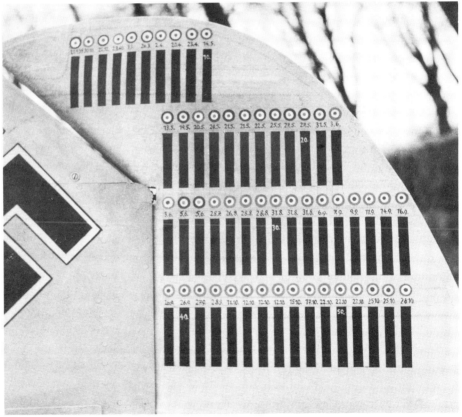

◄ Colleagues help a *IV/ JG 51* pilot out of his Bf 109E-4 after combat with British fighters over the Channel.

◄▼ *Major* Adolf Galland is aided by his crew chief *Feldwebel* Meyer after a sortie over the British Isles.

► *Major* Galland's Bf 109E-4 taxies for take-off at Wissant, France, September 1940.

▼ Adolf *Galland* prepares for take-off in the summer of 1940. A veteran of combat in Spain, Galland proved to be both an excellent flight leader and a gifted tactician during the Battle of Britain.

▲ A former French airfield becomes home for men and machines of *JG 53* in 1940.

▶ The Bf 109 pilot's parachute also served as a cushion, fitting into the well of the seat.

▶▲A pilot wearing a clip of flare cartridges over his flying boots.

▶▼A Bf 109E-4, the standard *Luftwaffe* fighter during the early phase of the Battle of Britain.

◀ **Bf 109Es of *JG 27* *'Schlageter'* assemble for another mission, August 1940.**

◀▼**A fighter from *Jagdgeschwader 26* on patrol along the Channel coast, July 1940.**

▶ **Dornier Do 17s from *Kampfgeschwader 76* crossing the English coast, 13 August 1940.**

▼ **Heinkel He 111 bombers of *KG 53*, each carrying a bomb load of 4,410lb.**

◄ A Messerschmitt Bf 110 *Zerstörer* (destroyer).
► The Junkers Ju 88 long-range bomber played an important role during the Battle of Britain.

◄ A Junkers Ju 87B *'Stuka'* of *1/SG 1.*

► The main targets for the *Luftwaffe* bombers were RAF fighter bases, and this photograph shows the effect of a raid, with a Hurricane fighter in the foreground.

▲ The Spitfire was a dangerous opponent for the Bf 109, and aces like Robert R. Stanford Tuck, whose aircraft was shot down by flak, scored well during the Battle of Britain.

▼ Many German aircraft ran out of fuel before reaching their home airfields: the pilot of this Bf 109E-4 of *JG 51* barely reached the French coast after exhausting his limited fuel capacity – which allowed him to stay no more than twenty minutes over the target.

▶▲ A *Kette* of Messerschmitt Bf 109Gs of 7 *Staffel Jagdgeschwader 27* and *III/JG 27* over the Mediterranean in 1943.

▶▼*Oberleutnant* Joachim Müncheberg, *Staffelkapitän* of 7 *Staffel/ JG 26*, shot down nineteen Hurricanes over Malta. Here he is greeted with a wreath after returning to Gela in April 1941, again victorious in combat.

◄ While his Bf 109E-7 is re-armed and refuelled, *Oberleutnant* Müncheberg sits in his cockpit describing his latest mission to a captive audience.

► The first Bf 109Es of *1 Staffel/Jagdgeschwader 27* land at Ain el Gazala, 18 April 1941.

► *JG 27* flew most of its missions from Gambut and returned in the evenings to Gazala.

◄ The fighting over Malta was intense, and the pilots of *JG 26* took every opportunity to improve their skills and learn the tactics of their opponents, Spitfires and Hurricanes.

► The ground crew – always ready, always helpful – about to take their 109 over from the pilot and prepare it for another mission.

▲◄ Bf 109Es of *1/JG 27* over Gazala.

◄ The camouflage of a Bf 109E blends well into the brown-green desert below.

▲► *Hauptmann* Horst Cavganico, *Kommodore* of *II/JG 5 'Eismeer'*, had a Mickey Mouse painted on his Bf 109G-6. He scored 60 victories flying 600 missions, mostly in the East.

► Camouflage patterns varied greatly: this bomber-hunting Bf 109G on a soggy airfield has an unusual and distinctive scheme.

▲ Bf 109F *'Rote 3'* of *III Gruppe, 8 Staffel/JG 5 'Eismeer'* in 1943.

◀ *Oberleutnant* Heinrich Ehrler, *Kommandeur* of the famous *6/JG 5*, in the cockpit of his Bf 109F. Ehrler received his Knight's Cross on 21 October 1942 after 41 victories and finished the war with a score of 204 Russian aircraft.

▶▲The rudder of *Oberleutnant* Ehrler's 109F after 77 victories, Potsamo, Finland, 27 March 1943.

▶ Bitterly cold winter weather made daily operations extraordinarily difficult. Here, mechanics drape a cloth around the Daimler-Benz engine of a Bf 109F to retain some of the warmth being ducted from an oil sump heater.

▲ Bf 109Fs and a
Henschel Hs 126
reconnaissance aircraft of
JG 54 grounded by a
typical Russian blizzard.
◄ After the storm, the
aircraft are dug out of the
snowdrift and readied for
action.
►▲ A more permanent
airfield on the Eastern
Front. Elaborate log
revetments and steel mats
were a luxury not often
enjoyed by the pilots and
ground crews of *JG 5*.
► Pilots and mechanics
of *7/JG 26 'Rotherz'*
stationed at Gela, Sicily,
enjoy a change of pace in
the warm spring sunshine
of the Mediterranean,
1941.

◄ The *Luftwaffe* had many NCO pilots in their ranks. Here an *Unteroffizier* (Sergeant) poses in front of his Bf 109E-7.

▼ Originally stationed on the French coast, the 7th *Staffel* of *JG 26 'Schlageter'* was later transferred to Gela, Sicily, and eventually to Gazala, North Africa, in June 1941.

► Dark-skinned, blue-eyed Gerd Barkhorn, three years older than Erich Hartmann, finished his training just as the Second World War started in the autumn of 1939. Like most of the *Luftwaffe*'s 'old hands', he preferred the trusty Bf 109 to the newer Fw 190.

◄ Marseille receives congratulations from his mechanic for victories 49 and 50, qualifying him for the Knight's Cross.

◄▼After the mission, each encounter and victory is discussed and evaluated with fellow-pilots.

► *Hauptmann* (Captain) Gerhard Homuth, *Kommandeur* of 1/*JG 27* (and one of the high scorers in North Africa), graphically describes the location of one of his latest victims, March 1942.

▼ Hans Joachim Marseille inspects his latest victory. Although both the Hawker Hurricane and the Messerschmitt Bf 109 first flew in 1935, the latter was substantially superior in overall performance.

◄ A proud ace looks on as victories 49 and 50 are added to the red rudder of his Bf 109F-2.

▼ Horizontal engineering on the wing of a Bf 109 of 5/*JG 27*. The box on the windshield is a field telephone.

► While the pilot takes a short rest, Marseille's 'Yellow 14' is refuelled and readied for another mission.

►▼ Tailplane and rudder detail of a Bf 109 in the Western Desert.

128

◄ *Oberfeldwebel* Otto Schulz was one of the 'Top Guns' in North Africa. He scored 42 victories, from October 1941 until he was recorded as missing in action on 17 June 1942. Schulz received the Knight's Cross on 22 February 1942 for his 44th victory, the same day that Marseille received his.

▲ *Lt.* Marseille after returning from the mission in which he scored his 49th and 50th victories, which earned him the coveted Knight's Cross, awarded on 22 February 1942.

▼ The rudder of *Oberfeldwebel* Otto Schulz's Bf 109E after he had scored 20 victories, autumn 1941.

▲ The cockpit of a Bf 109G-10 featuring the so-called 'Galland hood' on which the framing was reduced to improve the pilot's vision out of the aircraft. The solid armour plate yielded to a framed, armoured glass panel, giving the pilot a view to the rear as well.

◄ A remarkable picture, taken via a telephoto lens, of a Bf 109G-10/U4 with a Galland hood and an IFF (Identification Friend or Foe) antenna behind the radio mast.

►▲ Final preparations before take-off for another mission against US bombers.

► Loading 20mm shells for a Bf-109F-4's MG 151 15/20 machine gun into their disintegrating link belts.

The fuselage-mounted MG 17 was based on the hand-held MG 15 machine gun and was synchronized to fire through the propeller arc at a rate of 1,100 rounds per minute. The MGs were staggered slightly fore and aft to allow the ammunition boxes (which each held 1,000 rounds) to be accommodated. Belts and spent shells were collected in the compartment below the boxes.

◄ The wing-mounted 20mm MG FF cannon of a Bf 109 are removed for maintenance.

▲ German fighters were noted for their heavy armament, particularly their slow-firing but deadly cannon. Here, maintenance personnel clean the barrel of a Bf 109F-2's engine-mounted 15mm MG 151/15, Russia, 1942.

▼ Adjusting the Revi optical reflector gun sight. The sight was padded by a rubber cushion to protect the pilot's head in the event of a crash landing.

◄ French workers rig a Bf 109G-14 for gun alignment.

▲ Aligning the engine-mounted MG 151/15. The 15mm Mauser MG was belt-fed and had a rate of fire of 700 rounds per minute, with a velocity of 3,430fs. Both breech covers are open.

▶ The pilot looks on while a logistics engineer measures the impact of the rounds on the target. The sign reads 'Stop! Shooting with live ammunition. Danger.'

▲ An 'Emil' on jacks and with its tail propped up for bore-sighting. The aircraft has a VDM constant-speed propeller; later models of the Bf 109 had paddle-bladed airscrews to improve climb rate and absorb increased engine power. ►▲ Armourers prepare a Bf 109E of *JG* 27 for another bombing mission against Malta. ►▼ A 550lb bomb is easily handled using a special hydraulic dolly.

▲ In addition to its bomb load, the Bf 109E-4/B was armed with two engine-mounted 7.29mm MG 17 machine guns and two 20mm MG FF cannon in the wings each fed by a sixty-round drum.

◄ The bomb is secured and is getting a final check by the crew chief.

►▲A Bf 109E-4/B takes off, its roaring Daimler-Benz DB 601A causing a stream of dust.

►► *Lt.* Steindl, *Geschwader-Kommodore* of *II Gruppe/JG 54 'Grünherz'*, in his Bf 109E-4B, with an ETC 500 bomb slung under the fuselage.

►▼A Messerschmitt Bf 109E of the *Gruppen Kommandeur, 1/JG 5 'Eismeer'*.

◄ An interesting photograph of a Bf 109E-4/B fighter-bomber with its landing gear doors removed to prevent the build-up of sludge during take-offs from snow-covered fields.

► A number of Bf 109Gs were fitted for the specialized *'Pulk-Zerstörer'* (bomber-formation destroyer) role. A pair of Wfr.Gr.21 (*Werfer Geräte*) mortars were carried under the wings.

◄ An ETC 50/VIIId bomb rack holding four SC 50 (50kg) bombs. The lettering on the rack reads *'Für Me 109E u. F.'*

► A Bf 109G-6/R6 *'Pulk-Zerstörer'*, March 1943.

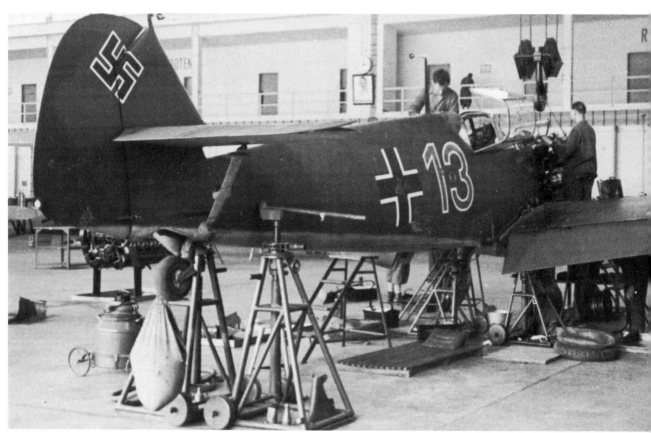

◄ Bf 109E-1 *'Rote 13'* of *JG 51* during factory overhaul in Augsburg, 1939.

◄▼ This Bf 109E-1 of *2/JG 26 'Schlageter'* had its three-bladed propeller damaged after the landing gear collapsed during take-off.

► A factory-fresh DB 605 engine is prepared for installation in a Bf 109 fighter.

▼ Removed from the Bf 109 airframe, a DB 605 powerplant is easily accessible for the mechanics.

◄ A Bf 109E-4 receives a brand new DB 601 engine.

▼ A well-worn DB 601 engine is removed from a Bf 109F of *5/JG 52* at an airfield on the Eastern Front, 1943.

► Mechanics from *5/JG 52* worked round the clock under primitive conditions to keep the strength of the *Geschwader* at the maximum possible at all times. Men like these made a major contribution to the achievements of their units.

►▼Mechanics of *1/JG 137* check the radio equipment of a Bf 109C.

▲ The L-shaped aluminium fuel tank of the Bf 109E held 400 litres. A 92-octane grade fuel was the norm for German fighter aircraft; here, the yellow triangle adjacent to the filler indicates a minimum grade of 87.

◄ The white spiral on the red spinner gave a slow, 'jumping' effect to an enemy gunner when approached head-on, thus throwing him off his aim.

► A Bf 109F-5 reconnaissance aircraft with engine cannon removed is fitted with cameras and film container. A 66 Imp. gallon drop tank is slung under the fuselage.

▶ A supply of 300-litre (66 Imp. gallon) standard auxiliary fuel tanks. The *Rüstsatz* R3 was fitted on all Bf 109G and K versions.

▼ *Jabos* (fighter-bombers) of *Jabo-Staffel/ JG 27* during operations against British shipping in the Mediterranean.

Appendices

Bf 109E-0	Powered by DB 601A-1 engine with fuel injection, providing 1,050hp at take-off. Armament four MG 17s, two in wings and two in cowling. Ten pre-production machines built.
Bf 109E-1, E-1/B	Production aircraft. Same as E-0, except MG 17s in wings replaced by MG FF 20mm cannon. E-1/B modified to carry a 50kg bomb.
Bf 109 V17	Powered by DB 601Aa of 1,175hp and with provision for engine-mounted MG FF cannon.
Bf 109E-3	Same as V17. Production aircraft.
Bf 109E-4	Redesigned canopy and armour (non-existent in earlier versions). Two MG 17s, two MG FF/Ms.
Bf 109E-4/B	Fighter-bomber. Same as E-4 with added ability to carry up to 250kg of bombs on fuselage.
Bf 109E-4/N	Same as E-4 but powered by a DB 601N engine with increased compression and utilizing higher octane fuel.
Bf 109E-4/Trop	Tropicalized by adding dust filter over supercharger intake and survival kit in fuselage behind pilot.
Bf 109E-5	Armed reconnaissance fighter. Four MG 17s. No wing armament. Carried a single camera.
Bf 109E-5/N	Same as E-5 but featuring DB 601N with higher compression. Also called Bf 109E-6.
Bf 109E-5/Trop	Tropicalized E-5 with survival kit and dust filter.
Bf 109E-6	See Bf 109E-5/N. Four MG17s.

▼ **Two Bf 109F-5s serving with a long-range reconnaissance unit at a northern French base in January 1943.**

Bf 109E-7	Same as Bf 109E-4/N, with fuselage shackles for either a 300-litre fuel tank or 250kg of bombs. Two MG 17s, two MG FF/Ms.
Bf 109E-7/Trop	Tropicalized E-7 with survival kit and dust filter.
Bf 109E-7/V2	E-7 with additional fuselage armour for protection in close-support role.
Bf 109E-7/Z	E-7 with nitrous oxide fuel additive (GM 1 unit) for emergency boost.
Bf 109E-8	Long-range fighter. Same as E-7 but with DB 601E, producing 1,350hp at take-off. Some E-8s fitted with skis on trial basis.
Bf 109E-9	Same as E-8 but used as photo-reconnaissance aircraft. No wing armament; single camera behind pilot.
Bf 109T-0	Bf 109E-1 modified for shipboard use (*Träger*, or carrier). Extended wingspan, with upward-hinging wings for onboard stowage, and arrester hook. Ten E-1s converted to T-0s.
Bf 109T-1	Powered by DB 601N. Sixty completed, but naval equipment subsequently removed. Built by Fieseler.
Bf 109T-2	Designation for Bf 109T-1 with shipboard fittings removed.
Bf 109F-0, V21	Ten pre-production aircraft, each with its own V number. Featured aerodynamically improved fuselage shape and horizontal tail, with smaller wing area, but retained square wing tips of earlier Bf 109s.
Bf 109 V22	As above but with DB 601E engine.
Bf 109 V23	Redesigned supercharger intake (eventually standardized), new wing flaps. Wing armament discarded.
Bf 109 V24	Same as V23 but without new wing flaps. Single MG 151 fitted to fire through propeller hub.
Bf 109F-1	Production aircraft, with rounded wingtips. DB 601N engine. Two MG 17s on upper cowling and one MG FF/M firing through propeller hub.
Bf 109F-2	Same as F-1 but with MG 151 15mm gun replacing MG FF/M.
Bf 109F-2/Trop	Tropicalized F-2 with dust filters and survival kit.
Bf 109F-2/Z	F-2 with the nitrous oxide (GM 1) pack added.
Bf 109F-3	Basically as F-2. DB 601E engine with lower fuel octane requirements. Two MG 17s, one MG 151/20.
Bf 109F-4	As F-3. Engine-mounted cannon changed from 15mm MG 151 to 20mm MG 151. Revised cockpit armour.
Bf 109F-4/B	Fighter-bomber version of F-4 with shackles for 250kg of bombs under fuselage.
Bf 109F-4/R1	F-4 with *Rüstsätze* (conversion units) – two 20mm MG 151 cannon in gondolas under wings, one 20mm MG 151 cannon firing through propeller hub, and two MG 17s in cowling.
Bf 109F-4/R6	F-4 fitted with special shackle, similar to that of F-4/B, for fighter-bomber role.
Bf 109F-4/Trop	Tropicalized Bf 109F-4, with dust filter and survival kit.
Bf 109F-4/Z	Bf 109F-4 with GM 1 nitrous oxide pack.
Bf 109F-5	Armed reconnaissance fighter. Same as F-4, but engine-mounted cannon removed and camera added. Two MG 17s.

▲ **A Bf 109G-6 taking off to intercept B-17 bomber formations. A 300-litre fuel tank has been left on the field.**

Bf 109F-6   Unarmed photo-reconnaissance aircraft. Special bay installed to house interchangeable cameras.

Bf 109 V30   F-1 airframe with cabin pressurization and air-conditioning systems for Me 309.

Bf 109 V30a   As V30.

Bf 109 V31   F-1 with a semi-retractable oil cooler and inwardly retracting, wide-track landing gear.

Bf 109G-0   Pre-production series. Fitted with DB 601E engine, though cowlings designed to accept as yet unavailable DB 605A of slightly different shape and with longer oil cooler. Pressurized cockpit.

Bf 109G-1   Production series. Same as G-0 but fitted with DB 605A. One 20mm MG 151 in nose and two MG 17s in cowling. Provision for GM 1.

Bf 109G-1/Trop   Two MG 17s replaced by two MG 131s, necessitating breech cover bulges. Fitted with tropical dust filters and survival kit.

Bf 109G-2   As G-1 but without cabin pressurization or GM 1 pack. Two MG 17s, one MG 151/20.

Bf 109G-3   As G-1 but with different radio gear. Two MG 17s, one MG 151/20.

Bf 109G-4   As G-2 but with different radio gear.

Bf 109G-2/R1   G-2 fitted with two 300-litre fuel tanks under wings, plus shackle under fuselage for carrying 500kg bomb. Large, jettisonable tail wheel fitted just aft of pilot's seat.

Bf 109G-5   First series fighter with MG 131s and gun 'bumps'. Fitted with either new DB 605AS engine (additional supercharging) or standard DB 605A. Provision for cabin pressurization.

Bf 109G-5/U2   First of G series to employ all-wooden vertical tail surface of increased height and area. ('U', for *Umrüst-Bausatz*, designates a modification to the airframe, as distinguished from a *Rüstsatz*, which adds something to it.)

▲ Messerschmitt Bf 109G-6/N *Werk Nr.* 27412 equipped with a FuG 350 Naxos-Z electric receiver for homing in on RAF H2S radar.

Bf 109G-6	First standard G-series aircraft designed to allow for field modifications. No cabin pressurization. Standard armament one 30mm MK 103 cannon or one MG 151 in nose, plus two 13mm MG131 machine guns in upper cowling. DB 605A or AM engine, and later DB 605D, with water-ethanol injection (MW 50) system in place of GM 1 nitrous oxide pack.
Bf 109G-6/R1	Bf 109G-6 fitted with *Rüstsatz 1* (shackles for carrying a 250kg bomb, plus battery box for fusing it).
Bf 109G-6/R2	Bf 109G-6 with *Rüstsatz 2* (pair of Wfr. Gr. 21 rocket mortars under wings).
Bf 109G-6/R4	G-6 with *Rüstsatz 4* (pair of 30mm MK 108 cannon mounted in streamlined gondolas under the wings).
Bf 109G-6/R6	Mk 108 cannon of R4 variant exchanged for MG 151s 20mm under wings.
Bf 109G-6/U2	Same vertical tail surfaces as G-5/U2. Could be fitted with either R4 or R6 armament system.
Bf 109G-6/U4	Semi-retractable tail wheel added, to reduce drag.
Bf 109G-6/U4N	Standard G-6/U4 developed for *Wilde Sau* night interceptions, with IFF transceiver for night identification to ground and other air units. Many equipped with R4 armament.
Bf 109G-6/N	*Wilde Sau* night fighter, armed to G-6/R4 standard. Featured FuG 350 Naxos-Z radar set, with antenna mounted inside clear plastic dome on top of fuselage behind pilot.
Bf 109G-6/Trop	G-6 fitted with standard tropical filter and survival kit.
Bf 109G-7	G6 with wooden tail surfaces of G-6/U2 and semi-retractable tail wheel of G-6/U4. Very few produced.
Bf 109G-8	Armed reconnaissance fighter with DB 605A-1 or DB 605AS engine. Cowling-mounted MG 131s removed and troughs faired over, leaving only the engine-mounted MK 108. Bay provided for interchangeable cameras.

Bf 109G-10	Featured the new DB 605D engine for low-octane fuel, or DB 605DB for high-octane fuel, both producing about 1,800hp at take-off. Armed with either a 30mm MK 108 or a 20mm MG 151 in nose, as well as two MG 131 machine guns in upper cowling. New radio equipment and provision for 300-litre fuel tank. Aircraft fitted with DB 605DC had MW 50 water-methanol injection system. All G-10s had 'Galland hood' canopy.
Bf 109G-10/R1	G-10 fitted with the R1 *Rüstsatz* (bomb shackles for 250kg bomb, and bomb-fusing battery box).
Bf 109G-10/R2	Standard G-10 converted to a high-speed reconnaissance fighter by installation of DB 605DB and camera bay, and deletion of cowling-mounted MG 131s.
Bf 109G-10/R4	G-10 with standard R4 armament modification.
Bf 109G-10/R6	G-10 with R6 armament modification.
Bf 109G-10/U2	G-10 with G-6/U2 modifications. Could be armed as either G-10/R4 or G-10/R6.
Bf 109G-10/U4	G-10/U2 with retractable tail wheel. Armed as R4 or R6.
Bf 109G-12	Unarmed, two-seat trainer version of Bf 109G. Many G-5s and G-6s converted to this configuration.
Bf 109G-14	Fitted with DB 605AM (with the MW 50 injection system), or the DB 605A, DB 605AS, DB 605ASB, DB 605ASM or DB 605D. Two MG 131s and one MG 151/20mm cannon. Provision made for now-standard field modifications.
Bf 109G-14/R1	G-14 with the R1 modification allowing for carriage and arming of 250kg bomb in flight. Additional undersurface armour added for engine and pilot protection.
Bf 109G-14/R6	G-14 with the standard R6 armament modification.
Bf 109G-14/U4	G-14 with the extended wooden tail surfaces.
Bf 109G-16	G-14 with standardized DB 605D engine, additional engine armour and provision for the R1 and R6 modifications.

▶ A Bf 109G of *JG 2* is refuelled from an Opel Blitz tank truck. A water bucket is placed under the fuselage to catch any overflowing fuel.

◀ A Bf 109G-10/R6 of *JG 3*, in France. The 20mm MG 151 cannon installed in gondolas under the wings were each provided with 120 rounds of ammunition.

Bf 109 V49, V50, V54, V55	Predecessors of Bf 109H series. Designed for high-altitude reconnaissance above 40,000ft.
Bf 109H-0	Originally a Bf 109F-4/Z, with cabin pressurization, extended wing span, wide-track undercarriage and extended tailpane. Provision for camera bay in the fuselage.
Bf 109H-1	G-5 fuselage with cabin pressurization, same wing and tail modifications as H-0, and DB 605A engine with GM 1 nitrous oxide pack.
Bf 109H-2	The so-called 'heavy high-altitude fighter'. As H-1, but with two 20mm MG 151s and three 30mm MK 108 cannon.
Bf 109H-3	The 'light high-altitude fighter'. Similar to H-2 but with two MG 131s and one 20mm MG 151.
Bf 109H-4	Unarmed reconnaissance aircraft. Basically an H-1.
Bf 109K-0	Aerodynamic refinements made to G-14 fuselage. Cowling enlarged to accept either the larger DB 605ASCM or the DB 605ACM with GM 1 nitrous oxide pack as well as two MG 151 cowling-mounted guns. Engine-mounted cannon remained 30mm MK 108. Only a few built; served as pre-production aircraft.
Bf 109K-2	First production variant of K series. As K-0.
Bf 109K-4	As K-2 except for addition of cabin pressurization and installation of the more slowly firing 30mm MK 103 gun in place of MK 108.
Bf 109K-6	As K-4 except for addition of MK 103 guns under wings. Only a few saw service.
Bf 109K-14	Last series version. New DB 605L engine with two-stage supercharger gave 1,700hp at take-off, but provided a speed of 460mph at 38,000ft. Armament as K-4.

APPENDIX II: ORGANIZATION OF LUFTWAFFE UNITS

The organization of *Luftwaffe* fighter units generally followed the patterns established throughout the entire air force. From the smallest operational unit, the *Staffel*, this organization led upwards through the *Jagdgruppe*, the *Jagdgeschwader*, the *Jagddivision*, the *Jagdkorps* and, finally, the *Luftflotte*.

The *Staffel* was the smallest operational unit. The number of aircraft within this unit could be as low as five or as high as twenty but was generally nine. For tactical purposes the aircraft were further divided into groups of five (a *Schwarm*), three (a *Kette*) or two (a *Rotte*). The unit was commanded by a captain or lieutenant, known as the *Staffelkapitän*.

Three *Staffeln* formed a *Gruppe*, although fighter units usually had four *Staffeln* per *Gruppe* after a change made in the autumn of 1940. The commander, a major or captain, was known as the *Gruppenkommandeur* and had a small operations staff comprising a medical officer, an adjutant, a technical officer and an operations officer. The aircraft complement of the *Gruppe* ranged from 27 for a normal *Luftwaffe* unit to 36, four fighter *Staffeln* of nine machines each. In addition to these, three, the staff officers' aircraft, made up the *Stabskette*. The *Gruppe* was the basic combat unit of the air force.

Three *Gruppen* made up the largest homogeneous formation in the *Luftwaffe*, the *Geschwader*, and as fighter units were expanded a fourth or fifth *Gruppe* was attached to some but not all *Jagdgeschwader*. Command was exercised by an *Oberst* or *Oberstleutnant* (colonel or lieutenant colonel), known as the *Geschwaderkommodore*. His staff included officers for the duties of adjutant, operations, technical matters, signals or communications, organization, meteorology and intelligence. At full strength the *Geschwader* would count between 108 and 180 aircraft, excluding the headquarters flight (*Stabsschwarm*) of from three to six aircraft. Not all the aircraft within the *Geschwader* were necessarily of the same type or, if the same type, the same model. Thus it was possible to find Bf 109s and Fw 190s mixed within the same *Geschwader* or, in the case of the night fighters, 109s and Me 110s.

The *Jagddivision* and *Jagdkorps* functioned as fighter commands, while all such air force units organized into tactical and territorial air commands were known as *Luftflotten*, each of which would be assigned a particular command area and could be moved as necessary. The *Luftflotte* was the highest operational field headquarters and controlled not only the operations of its flying units but those of ground service units as well. The next higher command structures were the Air Ministry, the *Oberbefehlshaber der Luftwaffe* (the Air Force Commander-in-Chief, *Reichsmarschall* Göring), the OKW, and finally the Supreme Commander (Hitler).

A brief resumé of German unit identification may be helpful. The type of *Geschwader* is shown by its abbreviation. Thus '*JG*' indicates a *Jagdgeschwader*, equipped with single-engined fighters; '*NJG*' stands for *Nachtjagdgeschwader*, with night fighters (single- or twin-engined); '*ZG*' stands for *Zerstörergeschwader*, with heavy fighters (twin-engined); and '*KG*' denotes *Kampfgeschwader*, with bomber aircraft. Other *Geschwader* included those for Stuka and ground support units, reconnaissance units, transport units and maritime units. The abbreviation would then be followed by the *Geschwader*'s number, an arabic numeral, which were not necessarily in consecutive order. The *Gruppen* of a *Geschwader* were numbered consecutively in roman numerals. Thus *I/JG 1*, *II/JG 2* and *III/JG 2* represented the first, second and third *Gruppen* of *Jagdgeschwader 2*, a traditional fighter unit also known as the '*Richthofen*' *Geschwader* and earlier designated *JG 132*. The individual *Staffeln* of a *Geschwader* were consecutively numbered in arabic numerals 1 to 9, with numbers 1, 2 and 3 belonging to *Gruppe I*, 4, 5 and 6 to *Gruppe II* and 7, 8 and 9 to *Gruppe III*; in *Jagdgeschwader* possessing four *Staffeln* in each *Gruppe*, 5, 6, 7 and 8 would compose *Gruppe II*. When the *Staffel* number is indicated with the unit designation, the *Gruppe* number is understood and omitted. Thus the eighth *Staffel* of *JG 54* (nicknamed '*Grünherz*') is written *8/JG 54* and known to belong to *Gruppe III*. Fighter units which featured five *Gruppen* would contain twenty *Staffeln*, but the divisions would follow the system outlined above.

APPENDIX III: BF 109 WEAPONS SYSTEMS

Guns and rockets

Designation	Calibre (mm)	Manufacturer	Velocity (fs)*	Rounds per Minute (cyclic)	Remarks
MG FF	20	Oerlikon†	2,300 (700)	550	Used in C, D and E series. Electro-pneumatic cocking mechanism. Drum-fed.
MG FF/M	20	Oerlikon†	2,300 (700)	550	Standard MG FF with special mounting for attachment between cylinder banks of inverted-vee engine. Used on B, C, D and E series. Both belt- and drum-fed.
MG 17	7.92	Rheinmetall	2,980 (905)	1,180	Used in B, C, D, E and F series. Could be either mechanically or electro-pneumatically cocked. Belt-fed.
MG 131	13	Rheinmetall	2,475 (750)	930	Used in F, G and H series. Mechanical or electro-pneumatic cocking. Belt-fed.
MG 151	15	Mauser	3,430 (1040)	700	Used in F and G series. Mechanical or electro-pneumatic cocking. Belt-fed.
MG 151/20	20	Mauser	2,600 (790)	750–800	Used in F, G, H and K series. Mounted on engine or in R4 weapons modification packs. Mechanical or electro-pneumatic cocking. Belt-fed. Unsynchronized.
MG 151/20S	20	Mauser	2,600 (790)	500–700	As above except for rate of fire. Synchronized version cut down vibration to airframe.
MK 103	30	Rheinmetall	3,140 (860)	440	Carried mostly by Ks. Although slower, fired heavier projectile than MK 108.
Mk 108	30	Rheinmetall	1,720 (520)	660 (later 860)	Used in G, H and K series, either engine-mounted or in R6 weapons pack under wings. Belt-fed.
Wfr. Gr. 21	210	DWF	990 (300)	Single load	Aerial rocket. Powered by a 40lb solid propellant charge, with 90lb high-explosive warhead. Range about ¾ mile. Used in R2 weapons pack.

Bombs

Designation	Approx. weight (lb)	Type	Use
SC 10	4.4	Fragmentation	Anti-personnel.
SD 2	6.5	Fragmentation	Anti-personnel. Carried in large cluster canisters, 90 SD 2s in each.
EB or EB-1	2.2	Incendiary	For use on combustible targets. Used during the Battle of Britain.
SC 50	110	General purpose (high explosive)	Carried by Bf 109 fighter-bombers, four to a rack.
SC 250	550	General purpose (high explosive)	Standard load for R1-modified fighters.
SC 500	1100	General purpose (high explosive)	Carried only by a few specially modified Bf 109s with the large jettisonable tailwheel.

* Figures in parentheses denote metres per second.
† Oerlikon allowed for licence manufacture in Germany.

◄ **An ETC 500 rack is readied for loading a SC 250 bomb.**